Product Development and the Environment

The Design Council

The Design Council is the UK's national authority on design. Its main activities are:

- commissioning research on design-related topics, particularly stressing design effectiveness to improve competitiveness;

- communicating key design effectiveness messages to industry and government; and

- working to improve both design education and the role of design in education generally.

The Design Council is working with Gower to support the publication of work in design management and product development. For more information about the Design Council please phone 0171 208 2121. A complete list of book titles is available from Gower Publishing on 01252 331551.

Product Development and the Environment

Paul Burall

The Design Council
Gower

Published by
Gower Publishing Limited
Gower House
Croft Road
Aldershot
Hampshire GU11 3HR
England

Gower
Old Post Road
Brookfield
Vermont 05036
USA

Paul Burall has asserted his right under the Copyright, Designs and Patents Act 1988 to be identified as the author of this work.

British Library Cataloguing in Publication Data
Burall, Paul
    Product development and the environment
    1. New products 2. New products – Environmental aspects
    I. Title II. Design Council
    658.5'75

ISBN 0-566-07659-4

Library of Congress Cataloging-in-Publication Data
Burall, Paul.
    Product development and the environment / Paul Burall.
        p.   cm.
    Includes bibliographical references and index.
    ISBN 0-566-07659-4 (hardcover)
    1. New Products. 2. Green products. I. Title.
    TS170.B87   1996
    658.5'75—dc20   95-40205
                                                                          CIP

Typeset in 11 point New Baskerville by Bournemouth Colour Press and printed in Great Britain by Biddles Ltd, Guildford.

Contents

List of tables

List of text boxes

List of figures

Preface

Since writing my first book on the subject of product design and the environment just five years ago, a great deal has changed. At first sight, the issue has plunged down the list of priorities for designers as recession has swept environmental stories from the front pages of the press and from the top of the list of political priorities.

But look a little deeper and it rapidly becomes clear that, as far as industry and business is concerned, Green issues have moved from being a subject for fashionable debate to become embedded in the central strategies of many companies (indeed, the very acceptance of the word 'Green' – in its environmental connotation – by the business world is significant). There is now a recognition that economic and environmental objectives are inextricably linked, that we have to move towards sustainable systems that do not overburden the earth's regenerative capacities or risk the collapse of all that we have achieved.

I will quote just two examples of the kinds of challenge that underline the reasons why environmental issues are important to those who design, make and sell products. The first is climate change caused by the emission of global warming gases. No longer is this the subject of any real dispute – world leaders have accepted that the risks are so immense and tangible that action must be taken to reduce such emissions; insurance companies are already acting to protect themselves from the results of climate change; and industries involved in energy generation and use are devoting huge resources to developing cleaner and more efficient technologies.

The second example is that of pollution from vehicles. Once again, it is the firming of evidence of damage – this time directly to human health as well as to the general environment – that is forcing action, driving everything from the development of alternative fuels to sophisticated filters for diesel engines.

Another important change in the last five years is that many of the vague ideas for solutions being discussed then are now being turned into practical action. Recycling is no longer just a nice idea – industries are setting up organisations to collect and recover materials; companies have working systems in place for their products; and the Chicago Board of Trade – the world's largest futures exchange – has set up an exchange for trading recyclable materials.

But perhaps the most significant change is that business now realises that what makes environmental sense generally also makes business sense. There are two reasons for this. First, it is clear that the markets for clean technologies and clean products are those that are growing rapidly – the commercial opportunities are huge. Second, the objective of minimising waste and pollution is the same as maximising efficiency – indeed, the UK government's Advisory Committee on Business and the Environment has suggested that waste minimisation should be rechristened Total Process Efficiency.

For the readers for whom this book is primarily intended – managers, designers and others in business concerned with product development – perhaps the most important change is in the practicality of implementing a Green product design strategy. There have been substantial strides in the development of the tools, knowledge and techniques needed to develop products that meet environmental criteria. There are guidelines and standards. And there is a sophisticated market demanding products and services that satisfy both user and environmental requirements.

I hope that this book will assist in the development of the more environmentally-benign product designs that are essential if we are to achieve a sustainable future.

Paul Burall

1 Why environmental issues matter

- Introduction ■ The environmental driving forces
- Growing demand for environmental responsibility

Introduction

Public interest in environmental issues has been growing steadily since the 1960s. In the early days, this interest scarcely touched the design and product development aspects of business, although soft drinks manufacturers were targeted in the 1970s over their use of non-returnable bottles, while the nuclear power industry has long had to cope with doubts about the safety of reactors and the disposal of waste. More recently, the car industry has had to accept a variety of regulations aimed at meeting increasing concerns about pollution.

Companies in countries such as Germany and the Netherlands have been well aware of the importance of environmental issues for many years. For example, the major Dutch manufacturer Philips Consumer Electronics has been addressing general environmental issues for some 25 years, although it only began to look at environmentally-oriented product development comparatively recently. The company has now developed an Environmental Design Manual and is integrating environmental considerations into procedures, practices and mind-sets throughout the organisation (more information about the Philips approach is given later).

In the UK, it was not until the late1980s that environmental issues came into any real prominence in business circles. Then, the awareness of UK companies of the potential impacts on the environment grew rapidly amid what became a media environmental frenzy. Aerosol manufacturers who had never previously thought that the ozone layer was of any concern to them were rapidly forced to drop CFC propellants in the face of proof that the chemical was destroying one of the earth's critical protective features. Battery makers were obliged to cut the heavy metal content of their products. Detergents, petrol, tinned tuna, paper, light bulbs, packaging, toilet rolls, and so on, all became the subject of Green warfare as manufacturers fought for the newly environmentally-aware consumers.

Then came recession and environmental issues sank down the business and public agenda. For many manufacturers, product development itself became something of a luxury as they devoted all their energies to surviving today rather than winning tomorrow; environmental influences evaporated for all but those in the front line, such as the chemicals and automotive industries. As for the public, many people had learned that being Green was not quite as easy as it first appeared: some so-called Green products performed less well than their conventional rivals; doubts about the validity of many Green claims became apparent; and tighter purse strings dissuaded many from spending the extra demanded for some Green products.

Of course, business – at least in much of the English-speaking world – has become used to the shooting stars of the latest fad. Often generated by politicians or management gurus seeking to make a mark by highlighting some newly-fashionable concern – a very specific aspect of industrial relations, communications, safety, technology or whatever – and promoting this as a cure-all, such vogues last a few months and are then replaced by a new fad. Sometimes these fashions leave behind a useful remnant of new knowledge or improved performance; sometimes they disappear without trace. Who remembers the UK government's 1960s tribology campaign which set out to convince us that better lubrication was all that was needed to reverse its country's economic decline?

There are those who believe that environmental issues were just such a passing phase in the business and product development scene, that a little more recycling of bottles and tins and paper combined with measures to reduce poisonous factory effluents would keep Green concerns on the back burner.

High on the agenda

This chapter sets out to demonstrate that such assumptions are ill-founded. Indeed, for many companies environmental issues are already respectably high on the agenda. A survey carried out in 1993 by the Department of the Environment showed managers in large companies ranking environmental issues at eight out of 20 in their priority concerns list, above such issues as industrial relations, new technology and product rationalisation. For smaller companies, environmental issues were slightly less important, ranking eleventh. Companies ranging from Hoover and Digital Equipment to Marks & Spencer and the British Airports Authority are already committing substantial resources to minimising the environmental impacts of their activities, recognising that this is essential to their future success.

Environmental issues, far from disappearing into the background, have only just begun to cause what is an inevitable and profound process of change for business in general and for product development in particular. While the precise

---

Box 1.1 Hoover increases market share

In 1994, Hoover launched the first washing machine – the 'New Wave' – to win the new European Union Ecolabel endorsing its environmental credentials. The new machine rapidly trebled Hoover's share of the washing market in Germany and doubled its share of the premium market in the UK.

The 'New Wave' machine incorporates a range of design features aimed at minimising the use of energy, water and detergent. For example, instead of soaking the clothes in a bath of water, a spray action is used in order to minimise water – and, therefore, energy – use. A great deal of work also went into minimising the gap between the tub and the drum, again with the aim of reducing water use. Another feature is a valve that seals the tub so that no detergent is lost into the sump during washing.

The design team had to overcome the problem of achieving water reduction without infringing other manufacturers' patents; for example, Zanussi had pioneered a spray system in its Jetspray models. Hoover's designers achieved a similar result by incorporating a scoop system into the drum for distributing the water, thus overcoming the patents issue.

---

consequences of this process are impossible to forecast, it is clear that it carries with it both opportunities and risks. Companies and designers that see change as an opportunity for innovation and for meeting market needs in new ways are likely to prosper; those that resist change or misunderstand where change is leading may well go to the wall.

The environmental driving forces

One of the principal difficulties for managers trying to understand how environmental issues are likely to affect their particular business is that of timescale. For most companies, the short-term influences can be assessed with some certainty, provided that managers take positive measures to ensure that they analyse the direct environmental impacts of their operations and products and keep in touch with any changes in attitude in their particular markets.

In the longer term, environmental issues will radically alter business practices and markets, and managers planning strategies for the medium to long-term need to be aware of the direction in which these influences are leading. Only then can they begin to discern the far-reaching opportunities and dangers of what some see as the post-industrial revolution. So I will begin by outlining why change is inevitable and describe some of the key environmental driving forces in the hope that this will provide a framework within which managers and designers can construct their own assessment of the long-term implications for their own businesses and industries.

At one level, environmental issues are simply a progression of the health and safety concerns that have been a part of business life for a century or more. Thus companies are now expected to act to prevent damage from their activities not only within their own premises but downstream as well, this increased responsibility including all emissions to air, water or the ground and extending, to some extent at least, to the welfare not only of humans but also to other forms of life. More recently, this concept of responsibility has been enlarged still further to include the whole lifecycle of the products that the company makes. So far, this has tended to concentrate attention on what happens to products at the end of their life, with an emphasis on recycling. However, some industries are also finding pressure coming at the raw materials extraction end of their product lifecycles: for example, the paper industry has been under as much pressure from environmentalists for its supposed destruction of forests as for the desirability of recycling more paper, not least because the two are inextricably linked. Again, concerns about the rainforests have affected the use of tropical hardwoods for furniture and building components.

Measuring welfare

At another level, the whole way in which industrial economies operate is now being questioned. The traditional measure of economic success is Gross Domestic Product (GDP). This means that the overriding policy goal is to expand the total amount of economic activity, irrespective of the nature of the activity. Thus a dirty industrial process that produces a lot of waste and pollution may, in GDP terms, be more beneficial than an efficient, clean process, as the extra economic activity required to deal with the waste and pollution from the dirty process actually increases GDP. In the past, such apparent absurdities have not seemed to matter too much: after all, the extra activity does create jobs and wealth for someone, even if it brings no overall benefit to mankind.

Such perceptions are now changing. First, the costs of dealing with waste, of paying for energy lost through inefficiencies, and of meeting soaring health care expenditure caused by pollution-related illnesses are now beginning to eat into the benefits brought by increased economic activity. Using an Index of Sustainable Economic Welfare based on research carried out at the Massachusetts Institute of Technology, the UK-based New Economics Foundation (NEF) has suggested that the quality of life in the UK has begun to fall due to the cost of negative activities: according to the NEF, while GDP in the UK rose by 30 per cent between 1977 and 1990, 'welfare' fell by 4 per cent during the same period. This finding has since been reinforced by a MORI poll carried out in 1995 that showed that one in five people in the UK are rejecting materialism and 'conspicuous consumption' in favour of personal fulfilment and quality of life. This is four times as many adopting a 'post-materialist' view than 25 years ago and, according to MORI, is typical of a global shift in values which means that more people are now putting quality of life before economic issues.

More fundamentally, it has become apparent that economic activity in some crucial spheres has grown to such an extent that it is threatening the life support systems of the planet. Initially, environmentalists were concerned that non-renewable resources were being used up at such a rate that they would run out within the foreseeable future. Such fears have largely vanished (although they still apply in the long term to some resources, such as oil and gas), partly because new sources of depleting raw materials have been discovered and partly because technology seems capable of coming up with alternatives when scarcity threatens.

But while one environmental threat has faded, another has appeared that is, in many ways, far more serious. The new threat is from the waste and pollution caused by increasing economic activity. Some of these waste materials are now overloading the natural regenerative capacity of the earth to absorb them. The results of this overloading range from the local – the poisoning of rivers and lakes and erosion caused by intensive agriculture and the destruction of forests – to the global, such as the destruction of the ozone layer by CFCs and the risk of climate change caused by increasing emissions of greenhouse gases.

Environmental risks

While past rates of growth in economic activity and the consequent environmental damage have been extremely rapid – industrial production has increased 50-fold in the last hundred years – the trend is still accelerating, not least because previously undeveloped countries are fulfilling their natural ambitions to catch up with Western lifestyles. The potential for growth is enormous. The Western world has 20 per cent of the world's population but uses 80 per cent of the world's material and energy resources; even if the West stands still and the rest of the world grows only to the point of using half the resources per head used by the West, material and energy use will increase to two and a half times current levels. Until recently, this prospect would have been viewed with eager anticipation, for in simple GDP terms the growth rates envisaged appear hugely beneficial.

However, it is the environmental risks of such a scenario that are now beginning to dominate economic and political thinking. Climate change brought about by increasing emissions of greenhouse gases from such human activities as energy generation and transport threatens to inundate whole countries as well as forcing vast population migrations as fertile areas dry up; elsewhere, climate change will take an increasing share of the world's wealth in repairing storm damage, building flood defences and so on. While no one can yet forecast the exact consequences of climate change, the United Nations Environment Programme, in its 1994 *Environmental Data Report,* provided firm evidence for some effects having already become apparent: six of the seven warmest years since records began more than a century ago were in the 1980s and this trend is continuing into the 1990s; global mean sea level has risen at 1.8 mm a year over the last 60 years (equivalent to 7 inches a century); and most of the world's mountain glaciers have been in retreat over the last 100 years.

Counting the cost

Business is already beginning to see some of the costs of climate change. Munich Re, the world's largest reinsurance group, announced in 1994 that it was ending exposure in certain areas of business due partly to increased losses from unusually severe storms and floods attributed to climatic changes associated with global warming. Mr Wolf Otto Bauer, a director, said the company was 'convinced the global trend to more frequent and damaging catastrophes would continue over the long term. Munich Re places great stress on risk management and the signs that we are experiencing such a change in climate are increasing.' This followed losses by the company of more than $40 billion due to severe storms in the six years to 1993.

Climate change is not, of course, the only risk. The United Nations Environment Programme is also concerned about the stress being placed on natural renewable resources: each year during the 1980s, for example, 1 per cent of the tropical forests were felled, threatening 2–8 per cent of the planet's species with extinction within 25 years.

The extent of the challenge that these threats present is illustrated by the sort of environmental targets that are now emerging. The Intergovernmental Panel on Climate Change (IPCC) is calling for a 60 per cent cut in carbon dioxide (CO_2) emissions simply to stabilise CO_2 concentrations in the atmosphere and limit global warming. Dr Stephen Potter, Research Fellow in Design in the Open University's Design Innovation Group, has suggested that, to stabilise pollution at current levels while allowing for world GDP and population growth would require the amount of pollution per product to be cut in the next 20 years to around 10 per cent of current levels. Translating these ambitions into the improvement required in the performance of individual products underlines the extent of the challenge: for example, cars will have to achieve an average of 400 km per litre of petrol.

The efficiency revolution

Most people look at such forecasts and, even if they cannot fault the science, despair at the effects of such cuts on the quality of life. But there is a more optimistic view. Manus van Brakel, Coordinator of Friends of the Earth in the Netherlands, accepts that the developed world needs to reduce its consumption of natural resources by 75 per cent to achieve long-term sustainability. He recognises that telling people that they must cut their consumption by three-quarters is impossible but believes that there is, in practice, no need for the developed world to reduce its living standards. Instead, he suggests that current usage of resources is so wasteful that an 'efficiency revolution' could achieve both sustainability and equity. 'It is possible for seven billion people in the world to reach a consumption level and a standard of living compatible with corresponding current European levels just by using very efficient technologies', he told a meeting held alongside the Earth Summit in Rio de Janeiro in 1992.[1]

Sustainable development is increasingly being seen as the key objective. Sustainable development was defined in 1987 by the World Commission on Environment and Development chaired by Gro Harlem Brundtland (and popularly known as the Brundtland Commission) as being development which 'meets the needs of the present without compromising the ability of future generations to meet their own needs'.[2]

Implications for product development

Manus van Brakel's efficiency revolution, the concept of sustainable development, and the switch from GDP to some kind of welfare index as the key economic indicator all lead in the same direction as far as product development is concerned. For they all require a switch from a linear system of resource use –

where materials and energy are used and then cast aside – to a circular system that aims to minimise the throughput of energy and raw materials without sacrificing the well-being of people. In a circular economic system, the emphasis switches to making the most efficient use of resources and to recovering and re-using waste energy and materials so that as little as possible is lost from the system. Such an approach has the automatic effect of minimising pollution, for pollution is simply a form of waste lost from the system.

The implications for product development are, of course, far-reaching. Recycling has already become a major issue for some industries. This is hardly surprising when the waste thrown away in industrialised countries is quantified. For example, each person in the United States generates 720 kg of household waste every year; the UK figure, at 350 kg a year, is around the European Union average. Nevertheless, recycling is in many ways a relatively low priority in the changes needed to achieve an economically and environmentally sustainable future. Concepts such as materials minimisation, energy efficiency, repairability

---

Box 1.2 **Environmental issues and the furniture industry**

Among the environmental issues of concern to furniture designers are the selection of materials; recycling; product life extension; and airborne pollution. The damage to tropical rainforests from the extraction of timbers such as mahogany and rosewood means that these should be replaced with softwoods and temperate hardwoods such as oak and ash. Recycling should be assisted by marking plastics components for easy sorting. Where appropriate, furniture should be designed to simplify re-upholstery so that its life can be extended and changing fashions accommodated. Where possible, the use of glues, varnishes, lacquers, stains and paints containing organic solvents should be avoided, as these are toxic and have been associated with sick building syndrome.

Such influences are, of course, not unique to the furniture industry and these kinds of environmental considerations are now confronting manufacturers in almost every field of product development.

and long life are, in the long run, likely to prove far more critical.

Later in this book I will look at some of the wider implications for business of the moves towards sustainability, implications that may, for example, force manufacturing companies who currently see their role as designing, making and selling products to switch to a more service-oriented approach.

Such fundamental changes are, of course, unlikely to happen overnight. Of more immediate concern to the designers, engineers and managers responsible for product development are the pressures already building up to force companies to develop products that reduce environmental impact. The next chapter looks at the growing regulatory framework that is the prime motivator likely to affect product development in the near future. But first I will outline how environmental quality is becoming an ever-increasing factor in the choices made by the general public.

Growing demand for environmental responsibility

Consumer demand can, of course, be a key driving force for the development of more environmentally-friendly products. Among the public, there is ample evidence that consumers are, in principle, concerned about the environmental impact of their purchasing decisions. For instance, a survey of a thousand people carried out by Mintel in the UK found the proportion looking for Green products had climbed from 53 per cent in 1990 to 60 per cent in 1994, despite the recession. On average, consumers claimed to be willing to pay 13 per cent more for Green products, with women, managerial and professional groups and those aged between 35 and 44 willing to pay even more. Numbers claiming to be unaware or unconcerned about environmental issues fell from 18 per cent in 1990 to 10 per cent in 1994. Mintel's consumer research manager commented that Green consumerism had become firmly established as a mainstream market influence: 'Environmentalism has not gone off the boil. It has spread across a much wider range of consumer groups, ages and occupations.'[3]

But another study in the UK – carried out in 1993 by Nielsons, the world's largest market information group – suggested that price and performance considerations were still holding back the sales of some Green products. However, this study also concluded that consumers seemed increasingly to regard the availability of environmentally-friendly goods as an important factor when deciding where to shop. The study also found that three-quarters of all consumers bought recycled paper products and half took bottles to a bottle bank for recycling. The increasing concern for the environment and the growth in positive responses by the public is underlined by a 1994 survey carried out by the UK government (see Table 1.1).

But there is undoubtedly still a lag between intentions and practice. Even in Germany – where consumer awareness of environmental issues is far better established than in the UK – an expression of environmental concern does not always translate into action. For example, one study found that, although 68 per cent of car buyers considered themselves to be environmentally concerned, between 1985 and 1990 there had been virtually no improvement in fuel efficiency of cars as consumers were more interested in the gadgets, speed and image than the crucial environmental factor of fuel efficiency. This compared with the post oil crisis concern of the late 1970s when, due to public demand, the fuel efficiency of German cars increased by at least 20 per cent between 1975 and 1985.

Table 1.1 UK attitudes to the environment in 1994

General	Concerned	Not concerned
Public concern about the environment	85% concerned	14% not concerned
Selected issues	*Those worried*	*Those believing a lot could be done*
Destruction of tropical forests	80%	78%
Global warming	71%	65%
Chemicals in rivers and seas	92%	91%
Disposal of toxic waste	87%	85%
Traffic congestion	75%	60%
Litter and rubbish	76%	79%
Who should pay		
Polluter pays even if goods and services cost more		62%
Cut back in other areas of public spending		19%
Higher taxes		76%
Personal actions		*Done on a regular basis*
Make sure that their noise does not disturb others		77%
Recycling paper		48%
Recycling glass		44%
Cut down on car use for short journeys		26%
Deliberately use public transport instead of car		8%
Avoided using pesticides in the garden		57%
Used unleaded petrol		53%
Used recycled paper at home		45%
Bought phosphate-free washing powder		17%
Used low energy light bulbs in the home		16%
Bought organically-produced food		12%
Product information		
Do manufacturers provide enough environmental information on their products	No 88%	Yes 10%

Source: Department of the Environment

The energy imperative

The German attitude to cars may, though, be a little misleading. When it comes to buying refrigerators, energy efficiency is a prerequisite for most German buyers, unlike their ill-informed UK counterparts. This, in turn, has had a noticeable effect on competitiveness in the refrigerator industry, for German manufacturers have been forced to improve the efficiency of their products while UK manufacturers have felt no such pressure from their home market. As a result, UK-made refrigerators are so poorly designed that they use around twice as much electricity as German fridges. As a consequence, few German consumers will look at a UK fridge, while German manufacturers have been able to dump their more inefficient models into a gullible UK market. Significantly, Germany exports half of the refrigerators it makes while the UK exports only 13 per cent.

While consumer pressure is not yet the most powerful driving force for the development of products with reduced environmental impacts, its importance is likely to grow. The consumers of the future are extremely concerned about environmental issues and are far more knowledgeable than many of their elders. A government survey carried out in the UK in 1994 showed that 90 per cent of all children were worried about deforestation and polluted oceans and 86 per cent of 13–15 year olds were concerned about global warming.[4]

Changes in buying habits

There is also ample evidence of the rapid changes in buying habits that can be brought about by environmental scandals. For example, the sale of tinned tuna plummeted when tuna fishing was blamed for the deaths of dolphins. And there are a number of key environmental issues that could cause a rapid Greening of consumer attitudes. These range from forecasts from some scientists that climate change will denude much of eastern England of trees within two generations to evidence that the substantial drop in male fertility in the last 20 years could be due to household soaps and washing powders breaking down into oestrogen-like substances that accumulate in the environment.

The development of environmental labelling and the selective application of direct fiscal incentives aimed at changing behaviour will also encourage consumers to look increasingly for Greener products in the future. And the increasingly sophisticated regulatory framework described in the next chapter will further encourage awareness of environmental issues, as well as providing performance indicators that will, in many cases, be used as measures to be bettered rather than simply met.

2 Pressures for change

■ Introduction ■ Regulation ■ Voluntary action
■ Fiscal pressures

Introduction

While the pressure from the public for products that are more
environmentally friendly is an important influence on product
development, it is the growth in environmental legislation and
the development of formal standards and labelling schemes that
are of most significance. This chapter examines the main
mandatory and non-mandatory driving forces that are giving
increasing urgency to the development of products that minimise
environmental damage.

Regulation

Regulations imposed on business in the interests of
environmental protection can take a wide variety of forms and
range from the draconian to the almost-voluntary. Where the risk
is acute and proven, regulations can be imposed rapidly and
globally: the Montreal Convention to drastically curtail the
production of CFCs was signed in 1987 by the leading industrial
countries within about two years of final scientific proof that CFCs
were damaging the earth's protective ozone layer. At the other
end of the scale, local pressures can bring about local actions: for

instance, cars are banned from parts of Athens when pollution levels reach unacceptable levels.

What is more, the consequences of new regulations are not always immediately obvious to some of the businesses affected. Manufacturers of clothes using such materials as fur, leather, beads, feathers and other items marked 'Dry Clean Only' and qualified with an 'F' code feared that their garments could no longer be cleaned when the European Union agreed to ban the CFC-based solvent required for the cleaning process.

In 1993, the Australian Manufacturing Council published a report[1] examining the different kinds of environmental regulatory control that can affect businesses (see Table 2.1). All

Table 2.1 **Types of environmental regulatory controls**

Type	Description	Example
Co-regulation	Formulation and adoption of rules and regulations done in consultation with stakeholders, negotiated within prescribed boundaries	■ National registers
Economic instruments	Use of pricing, subsidy, taxes and charges to alter consumption and production patterns of firms and individuals	■ Tradeable permits ■ Tax incentives ■ Pollution charges ■ Deposit refund schemes ■ Resource cost pricing
Sanctions	Broad ambient standards setting using command and control instruments (licences), limited scope for flexibility	■ Air and water quality standards
Self-regulation	Initiatives by firms or industry sectors to regulate themselves through the setting of self-imposed standards, and involving monitoring of member firms to ensure compliance	■ Codes of practice ■ Self audit ■ Pollution reduction targets

Source: Australian Manufacturing Council, 1993

of these kinds of regulatory controls are being applied in different parts of the world, although the emphasis varies and, indeed, continues to shift quite rapidly. This means that environmental regulation presents two distinct challenges to business organisations: the first, of course, is to meet those regulations that are introduced; the second, and in many ways more difficult, is to discern how the regulatory framework is likely to develop and how this will affect their own industry and company in the future.

There are two main reasons why the approach to environmental regulations changes relatively rapidly. Both are due to the fact that this whole field is so new that understanding of what is needed from an environmental point of view and what works in practice is still developing. For example, early legislation to control pollution in the United States was based on controlling emissions to particular media – air, water or the soil. It rapidly became clear that this could be counterproductive, for industry became adept at switching its waste disposal from the controlled medium to one that was not controlled.

A look at how European Union environmental policy has developed will illustrate how regulatory thinking has changed over the last 20 years and will give some clues as to where the regulatory framework is now heading.

European Environmental Action Programmes

The first European Environmental Action Programme was introduced in 1973 and concentrated on cleaning up pollution. Its main importance was that it introduced the 'polluter pays' principle, placing the cost of cleaning up pollution clearly on those that cause it. This has been most effective in dealing with single major sources of pollution, such as chemical spills into rivers and oil spillages on coastlines. Elsewhere, the principle is difficult to apply because of the problems in pinning down the sources of many kinds of pollution and of attributing costs where many sources are each contributing a small amount.

The polluter pays principle is also used in support of other regulatory measures: for example, one argument for increasing the tax on petrol is that it is making the polluter contribute to meeting some of the costs of the consequent pollution. While originally envisaged as being of primary application to pollution resulting from manufacturing processes, the principle may become of greater significance to product developers as it is now being used to argue for the extension of liability to manufacturers for pollution caused by products during their complete lifecycle. At the moment, this is largely being applied to the disposal of products at the end of their life by, for example, insisting on collection and recycling strategies. In the future, such liability may extend to pollution caused by the product in use, which would, for some products, present a major challenge to manufacturers. With the form of approaching legislation far from clear, it is apparent that some major companies are becoming ultra-cautious and are planning for the toughest possible liability scenario as the best way of protecting their long-term interests.

While the first European Environmental Action Programme was concerned with clearing up pollution after it had occurred, the second and third programmes focused more on prevention and on the development of clean technologies. As part of these programmes, the European Community introduced the Environmental Assessment Directive requiring information to be provided on the environmental impacts of major development proposals; this was intended to enable such impacts to be taken properly into account by planning authorities when considering large industrial developments, road proposals or other major construction projects.

The main impact on business of these early developments in environmental legislation was to launch a huge expansion in demand for the equipment needed to clean up pollution. Thus the market has boomed for everything from environmental monitoring tools and catalytic converters for cars to systems for cleaning and recycling the water used in the paper industry and equipment to recover silver from photographic processes. Adrian Wilkes, Director of the UK Environmental Industries Commission, claimed early in 1995 that 'the new commercial goldmine for environmental technology and service companies is now materialising. The industry is expected to be worth £140 billion a year by 2000.'[2]

The second and third programmes also introduced another key concept – the 'precautionary' principle. This calls for action to minimise the risk of significant environmental damage even before any final causal link has been proved on the basis that some of the major environmental threats are potentially so damaging that to wait for final scientific proof is too risky. An example is global warming: while absolute proof that increasing levels of greenhouse gases in the atmosphere causes damaging changes to the climate is unlikely to be available until the turn of the century, world leaders agreed at the 1992 Earth Summit to begin to take tough decisions to limit greenhouse gas emissions on the basis that the potential damage makes inaction unacceptable.

The fourth European Environmental Action Programme – launched in 1987 to coincide with the European Year of the Environment – called for environmental considerations to be integrated into all other major policy areas of the Community. It thus completed the policy transformation from treating pollution and environmental damage as something to be dealt with after it has happened to a policy of trying to ensure minimum damage in the first place.

The fifth Environmental Action Programme

The European Union's fifth Environmental Action Programme was adopted in March 1992 and covers the period 1993–2000. It aims to set the EU on the path to sustainable development as defined by the Brundtland Commission and sets as the main objectives for its policy towards industry the improvement of resource management; the promotion of consumer confidence in environmental quality and choice; and the setting of EU standards for production processes and products. The programme is innovative in being primarily proactive, for it is underpinned by the Single European Act which, for the first time, provides a constitutional mandate for the EU to take environmental protection measures.

The fifth programme also breaks new ground by adding a third element to the EU's strategies for implementation. In addition to continuing to fund environmental projects and impose legislation from the centre, the programme adds a bottom-up approach requiring a three-sided partnership involving producers, consumers and policy makers. This is already leading to some significant developments, especially in the generation of industry responsibility groups that aim to head off detailed legislation in such issues as recycling. This is of considerable significance to product developers, providing both incentives and direct assistance for the development of more environmentally sustainable products.

Table 2.2 **Toughening the limits on diesel emissions**

European Union regulations for diesel cars (units are grams per kilometre)

Year of introduction	Hydrocarbons+nitrous oxides	Carbon monoxide	Particulate matter
1994	0.97	2.72	0.14
1995/6	0.9	1	0.1
1999	0.7	1	0.08
2000+	0.5*	0.5*	0.04*

* under discussion

The rapid evolution of the EU's approach has meant that the regulations that have actually been agreed and put into practice are somewhat piecemeal and are far from complete, despite there being some 300 already in place (sources of further information are given in the appendix at the end of this book). For some industries that have been in the front-line of environmental concerns – for example, the automotive industry (see Table 2.2) and the major electricity generators – EU action has been relatively comprehensive, especially in terms of limiting emissions. In other areas, long-cherished ambitions have foundered on the rocks of national self-interest and doubts about the acceptability by the public of some of the effects. Perhaps most notably, plans for an EU-wide energy tax aimed at encouraging overall energy efficiency and a switch away from the fossil fuels whose use creates greenhouse gases were put on one side in 1994 after several years of negotiation, although individual countries will be at liberty to introduce them from 1996.

However, the general direction of the regulatory framework within the EU is becoming clear. A look at some of the EU Directives that have come into force will serve to indicate the main areas that should concern product developers.

European Union Directives

The EU's moves to cut greenhouse gas emissions from the use of fossil fuels began in 1992 when minimum efficiency standards were set for domestic boilers. Also in the interests of energy conservation, an EU Directive making energy labelling mandatory for refrigerators and freezers came into operation in 1995. These initiatives reinforce the key importance for designers of maximising energy efficiency.

The trend towards ever tighter controls on the emission of key pollutants continues. For example, in 1994 the EU announced a new framework Directive for ambient air quality which will see increasingly tough standards laid down over the next 20 years for eight specified pollutants, including carbon monoxide and acid deposits.

The Packaging and Packaging Waste Directive adopted in 1994 decrees that between 50 and 65 per cent of packaging materials must, by 2001, be recovered for recycling or energy recovery through incineration. At least 25–45 per cent of all materials must be recycled; and at least 15 per cent of each separate material must be recycled.

Electronics waste

The Packaging and Packaging Waste Directive is undoubtedly the forerunner of action in other product areas aimed at 'avoiding waste and preventing depletion of the natural resource stock' as set out in the fifth action programme. Electronic waste has been identified as one of the priority waste streams by the EU, with suggestions that manufacturers will be forced to take back products at the end of their life and recycle them in order to eliminate the current practice of simply dumping such items in holes in the ground. The implications are profound: such a scheme could add 10 per cent to the cost of a television. So far there has been no agreement on an EU-wide scheme and manufacturers in a number of countries are trying to develop voluntary schemes to head off any heavy-handed legislation. At the same time, a number of countries have threatened unilateral action. The German government is, for example, looking again at enforcing a take-back scheme; the Italian Parliament considered a take-back Bill in 1993 and Denmark, France and Austria have also considered action on electronic products.

The scale of the problem is two-fold: quantity and complexity. The UK Industry Council for Electronic Recycling (ICER) estimates that around a million tonnes of consumer electronic equipment is thrown away in the UK every year. And the volume is set to grow rapidly: in 1994, France produced 1.3 million tonnes of electronic waste but sold 2.1 million tonnes of new electronic products. The ICER was set up in 1994 as one of a number of government-inspired producer responsibility groups and reflects the bottom-up, voluntary approach to achieving the objectives of the fifth environment programme, although it is likely to be underpinned by UK legislation. Elsewhere, individual companies have taken action. For instance, in Germany four companies, including Apple and Acer, have set up their own take-back schemes. Hewlett-Packard started a recycling initiative in 1991 and its plant in France now recovers 95 per cent of materials compared with 70 per cent when it started; disk drives are used as spares, circuit boards are refined to recover precious metals, plastic is stripped from copper cables, microprocessors and memory chips are used in electronic toys, high-grade plastics are recycled and low-grade plastics are incinerated for energy.

There are two key lessons for those responsible for product development from the electronic equipment experience. First, the equipment being designed today may be subject to new legislation aimed at reducing waste by the time it reaches the end of its life, with manufacturers having at least some responsibility placed on them for those old products. Second, meeting demands for recycling and re-use is far easier and cheaper if these factors have been taken into account at the design stage.

The industries vulnerable to these changes are varied. The Dutch government, for instance, has proposed setting up producer-responsibility organisations to oversee recycling for white goods, brown goods (vacuum cleaners, televisions and so on), paper, cars, packaging, car tyres, batteries, paint tins, photographic chemicals, plastics products used in building and lubricating oils.

National regulations

National regulations of relevance to product development vary from country to country, with nations such as the Netherlands leading the way. The Netherlands Environmental Management Act, for example, allows for the introduction of an obligation to charge deposits or provide a financial incentive to return products or packaging in the interests of waste prevention and re-use and also allows the control or even total prohibition of products in the interests of waste prevention. The Dutch Chemical Substances Act can control the concentrations and recovery of prescribed substances, while the Air Pollution Act allows the prohibition or control of appliances whose use leads to air pollution; the Noise Abatement Act does the same for noise. Finally, the Netherlands also has an Energy-Efficient Appliances Act allowing the prohibition or control of appliances in the interests of reducing the consumption of energy.

Helpfully, the Dutch government has also indicated which

products it views as priorities for action. The provisional list, published in 1994, includes T-shirts, umbrellas, refrigerators, cooking and baking appliances, audiovisual equipment, small electrical appliances, electric toys, washing machines and dishwashers, central heating equipment, furniture, sports goods and shower heads. Already intentions are being turned into actions: at the beginning of 1995, a 'collection fee' of around £100 was added to the price of all new cars to pay for the cost of processing it in an environmentally-friendly way at the end of its life.

The Swedish approach to environmental regulation varies from the quite specific to the all-embracing. In 1994, Sweden's Department of Energy Efficiency was calling for legislation to force computers to power down to just one watt after one hour of inactivity; more generally, the proposed Ecocycle Bill would give the government power to formalise producers' responsibilities for all products from the cradle to the grave.

Denmark has the usual regulations prohibiting certain substances outright or limiting their application in products; but it also has legislation providing for the introduction of specific product-related environmental policy measures.

Regulation in the UK

In the UK, regulation is generally still based on preventing direct health risks through, for example, the 1988 Control of Substances Hazardous to Health (COSHH) Regulations. COSHH has increased the need for both continuous safety checks and also for occupational health, safety and hygiene purposes. The 1990 Environmental Protection Act provides for the control of pollutants whose negative effects range from global warming to damage to plants and buildings or to human health. The pollutants covered include nitrous oxides, sulphur dioxide, carbon monoxide, volatile organic compounds (VOCs), suspended particulates, hydrochloric acid, hydrogen fluoride, chlorine, ammonia, heavy metals and dioxins.

Generally, the UK has argued for EU-wide regulation rather than imposing local controls, even where the former has proved difficult to achieve. Nevertheless, some national regulation is being imposed, although not always directly by the government. For example, in 1995, the Committee of Advertising Practice – which enforces advertising standards in the UK except for television and cinema advertising – outlawed the use of terms such as 'environmentally friendly' unless they are qualified or supported by convincing evidence. The UK has also begun to adopt some tougher national standards, such as amending the water by-laws in 1993 to reduce the amount of water used in toilets by setting a 7 litre per flush maximum. The 1995 Environment Bill also includes a clause placing a duty on the water industry regulator OFWAT not only to promote economic and efficient behaviour on the part of water and sewage undertakers but also to encourage efficient use by their customers. However, some legislation actually inhibits environmental objectives: for example, a product that is returned and refurbished to the same performance and life-expectancy standard as a new product still has to be marked as second-hand by law, thus inhibiting life extension through re-use.

Regulation in the United States

In the United States, the legislative picture is somewhat similar to Europe, with some central regulation combined with varied approaches in different states. Table 2.3 indicates the variation in approach.

Table 2.3 **Examples of local laws affecting product design in the USA**

State	Provision
Maine	Ban on multi-layered beverage containers
Parts of Michigan and Oregon	Ban on polystyrene foam packaging
10 states	Ban on toxic heavy metals in packaging
California	Mandatory reductions in volatile organic compounds in consumer products
13 states	Regulations on the use of certain environmental terms in labelling (e.g. 'recyclable')
10 states	Recycled content requirements for newsprint
4 states	Limits on mercury in household batteries
4 states	Requirements for manufacturers to take back and recycle rechargeable batteries
Connecticut and New York	Requirements for all batteries to be 'easily removable' from products

Centrally, the USA has the powerful Environmental Protection Agency (EPA). Originally concerned primarily with major single sources of pollution – such as leaking chemical waste dumps – the EPA is turning its attention increasingly to areas of direct concern to product designers. For example, in 1988, the EPA set a new energy efficiency standard for refrigerators that, at the time, was only being met by 6 of the 2,000 or so models on sale; manufacturers were given just three years to meet the new standard.

The extent of the EPA's impact on product design is shown by one of its more recent programmes. This targets lawnmowers, golf carts and even snow blowers on the basis that these kinds of relatively small powered devices are responsible for 10 per cent of the country's ozone and carbon monoxide pollution. The EPA has adopted a two phased approach. In the initial phase, manufacturers will have to alter the air/fuel ratio in engines so that they burn petrol more thoroughly: this comes into force in

1996. Later, tougher standards will be introduced requiring catalytic converters or other anti-pollution devices to be fitted; in addition, owners may be required to have tools regularly checked at government monitoring stations.

Regulation in Japan

Japan has, until recently, had a mixed record. It has led the world in terms of legislating for energy efficiency, largely because of its lack of indigenous fuel sources. More generally, its industries have been allowed to heavily pollute their local environment. But that is changing rapidly, with possibly profound implications for Japanese industrial competitiveness.

According to the Centre for Environment and Economic Development at the UK's Ashridge Management Research College:

> Japan may be developing a new model of 'Asian Environmentalism' which is more consensual, human-centred, technocratic and business orientated than Western models. While this would be anathema to many greens, a model which appears to reconcile sustainable development with increased living standards – as a number of Japanese experts believe to be possible – may be attractive to many nations in Asia and the Third World. It could also create significant competitive advantages for Japanese business.[3]

The regulatory framework in Japan is tightening but is also being developed with close collaboration between government and industry. Japan has long insisted that its major companies report publicly on their energy efficiency and that they employ energy managers. Japan's Basic Environmental Law sets out a framework for future environmental legislation, including product requirements for ecolabelling and recycling. A Law for

the Promotion of Utilisation of Recyclable Resources was adopted
in 1991: this forces manufacturers in certain industries to take
account of recycling requirements at the product design stage
and covers consumer electronics, cars and packaging. The
Japanese government has recently passed an Automobile Exhaust
Law that places new demands on the owners of cars to reduce
nitrous oxide emissions and has also set a mandatory target for
automobile manufacturers of improving the average fuel
efficiency of new cars by 8.5 per cent by 2000.

There are, of course, environmental regulations of various
kinds being introduced in many other countries, ranging from
far-reaching regimes in nations such as Germany to elementary
regimes in most developing countries. To describe these more
thoroughly would be to waste space, for the environmental
regulatory framework across the world is in many ways in its
infancy.

Incentives for innovation

There is, however, one important point to be made. At first sight,
regulation would appear to be anathema to product developers
and to business, constraining what designers can do and adding
cost. In fact, there are many who will argue the opposite. Klaus
Topfer, the highly-respected and long-serving German
Environment Minister, told a conference in London in 1993 that
'It is the bottlenecks that lead to technological innovation.
Creating bottlenecks by imposing higher environmental
standards is not intended to lead to higher costs but to
technologies that will overcome the problems at no increase in
cost.' Klaus Topfer gave as an example the development in Japan
of equipment to remove nitrous oxides from power station
emissions: this was a direct consequence of legal restrictions

imposed on emissions and resulted in technology that was later sold to Europe.

This positive approach to regulation is reflected elsewhere. Philips, a major electronics manufacturer, states in its Environmental Policy Statement that it 'will take the initiative, where necessary, to promote workable and improved codes of practice and effective laws and regulations'. Even smaller companies seem not to see environmental regulation as an enemy. A survey of small firms carried out in 1994 by the British Chambers of Commerce found 24 per cent of respondents complaining that the pace of environmental legislation affecting their businesses was too slow while only 8 per cent thought that it was too fast.[4]

In summary, environmental regulation has so far made comparatively little impact on product development, with the exception of some front-line industries such as vehicle manufacture and parts of the packaging industry. But such regulation will have increasing influence, especially in the areas of energy efficiency and waste reduction. Regulation can be a spur to product innovation and an opportunity to gain competitive advantage (see Figure 2.1 for an example of a new product generated by environmental pressures).

Voluntary action

Mandatory regulations are not the only ones of concern to those involved in product development. Some government regulation is ostensibly voluntary but can, in practice, be unavoidable. The American Environmental Protection Agency, for instance, introduced a voluntary energy efficiency standard for computers: voluntary it may be, but any manufacturer wanting to sell to any government agency has to meet the standard, thus making it virtually mandatory as the government and its agencies are major purchasers that cannot be ignored. Significantly, this voluntary standard is now being met by computer manufacturers world-wide.

Even non-government organisations have the potential for similar influence. In 1992, the Sierra Club Legal Defense Fund asked the California Judicial Council to force lawyers to use recycled paper on their submissions to courts. In the USA, lawyers are the biggest consumers of paper after the government, each lawyer using a tonne of paper a year.

Figure 2.1 **Recycling truck**

The recycling of domestic waste is becoming increasingly common and in some parts of the world is mandatory. This has generated a new market for purpose-designed trucks to collect separated refuse. The A-Series recycling truck manufactured by the Oshkosh Truck Company was designed to meet this need by the American consultancy, Renquist/Associates working with the manufacturer's product development team. The modular recycling containers are, like the rest of the truck, easy to clean. Special attention was paid to the critical areas of driver control and access, as the truck is driven both seated and while standing. Excellent sightlines enhance safety and the truck has been designed to give an image of cleanliness and efficiency. Sales in the first nine months topped half a million dollars. (Renquist/Associates.)

> **Box 2.1** Swiss retailers force biodegradability
>
> It is not only governments that can enforce environmental action. In Switzerland, retailers refuse to sell liquids that do not meet OECD biodegradability recommendations, a veto that is not backed by any legislation yet is just as effective.

Environmental labelling

Another voluntary but, nevertheless, powerful incentive for taking environmental factors into account in product development comes from the growth of environmental labelling schemes.

Although a large number of countries have developed their own labelling schemes – the German 'Blue Angel' scheme launched in 1978 being perhaps the best known – within Europe the emphasis is now on the European Union Ecolabel, introduced in 1994. The advantages of a common labelling scheme that is accepted throughout the Single Market are obvious.

The EU Ecolabel scheme has the twin objectives of encouraging business to improve its environmental performance and of providing consumers with a reliable indication of the products in each category that have the least impact on the environment during their complete lifecycle. The criteria that a product has to meet to be eligible for the Ecolabel varies from product category to product category: the examples of the criteria for washing machines and hairsprays given in Boxes 2.2 and 2.3 provide a good indication of what is taken into account.

By the end of 1994, the EU Ecolabel criteria had been finalised for washing machines, dishwashers, soil improvers and kitchen towels/toilet rolls; those for laundry detergents, hairsprays and light bulbs were going through the final stages of approval. Other

Figure 2.2 **EU Ecolabel**

The European Union Ecolabel, designed by the UK consultancy Newell and Sorrell, came into use in 1994. (Newell and Sorrell.)

product categories being worked on included insulation materials, T-shirts, batteries, paints and varnishes, shampoos, cleaning agents, household cleaning products, building materials, ceramic tiles, packaging materials, refrigerators, cat litter, shoes, ceramic crockery, glassware (table and decorative), deodorants, hairstyling aids and growing media.

Manufacturers should not assume that, just because a product category is on the EU list for development, its introduction is imminent. Delays have occurred for a range of reasons. One problem has been that individual countries have been given responsibility for developing proposals for specific products,

Box 2.2 EU Ecolabel criteria for washing machines

Three types of criteria are specified for the EU Ecolabel criteria for washing machines:

Key criteria, including:
- Maximum permissible electrical energy consumption per kg of washload for two specified standard wash tests.
- Maximum permissible water consumption per kg of washload for one specified standard wash test.
- Five per cent or less detergent loss during a standard test.

Best practice criteria, including:
- The machine must have clear markings identifying the settings appropriate to fabric type and laundry code.
- The machine must have clear markings identifying energy and water saving programmes and options.
- Clear instructions must be provided to the consumer covering various aspects of efficient operation appropriate to wash, water and other conditions.
- Polymeric components used in quantities greater than 50 g must carry a permanent material identification mark.

Performance criteria:
- Minimum standards of stain removal must be achieved in two specified standard tests.
- A minimum set rinse efficiency must be achieved.

Box 2.3 Draft EU Ecolabel criteria for hairsprays

The draft criteria for hairsprays include:
- Volatile organic compound (VOC) content must not exceed 0.72 kg per EPL.*
- No compound with a photochemical oxidation potential greater than that of n-heptane should be used.
- Ozone depletors are banned.
- The use of global warming agents is restricted.
- Limits are placed on dispenser weight and at least 80 per cent of the dispenser weight must be a single material.
- No fitness for purpose criteria are set, as no standard test exists; but expert evaluation is required, although a product may be judged unfit for use only if it is significantly inferior to the worst performers of all commercial brands on any one of five performance criteria.

*Equivalent Pump Litres (for aerosols, 1.5 litres counts as one EPL; for finger and air pumps, 1 litre of formulation counts as one EPL) these then being subject to agreement by the other nations. This has sometimes led to accusations that the proposed criteria favour the originating country's home industry: the criteria for ceramic tiles was being prepared by Italy but have been delayed after accusations that they were biased in protecting the Italian industry's energy-inefficient two-firing process. Technical problems can cause delays too: the scheme for cat litter is being held up by a lack of odour measurement tests.

In the longer term, businesses should also expect the basis of the EU Ecolabelling scheme to evolve. The standards set for each category are intended to encourage improvement while providing consumers with a reasonable choice: generally, the intention is to set standards that allow around 15–20 per cent of the products currently on the market in any one category to be eligible for the label. The intention is to tighten standards as improved products are introduced, thus maintaining the competitive pressure for further improvement.

But the EU Ecolabel is not graded: products either pass or fail. From the beginning, this has aroused criticism on three grounds: first, it limits the information available to the consumer. Second, smaller companies have argued that it inhibits innovation, as a new product that performs considerably better than its rivals but has only a small market share gains no advantage, as this product carries exactly the same endorsement as a more damaging product from a large manufacturer. Finally, for some product categories the lack of a graded system makes the scheme almost meaningless. For example, the European Lighting Council favoured a graded energy labelling system as the suggested label standard would mean that all compact fluorescent bulbs (CFLs) would qualify but no other kind of bulb; this would provide no incentive to improve conventional lamps and gives the consumer no inducement to buy better-performing CFLs.

Energy labelling

These pressures mean that the EU Ecolabel is likely to evolve in the medium term, probably both by introducing different grades of approval and by providing specific performance information. The pattern has already been partly set by EU Regulation 75/92, which is making energy labelling mandatory for household appliances. First implemented in the UK in 1995 for refrigerators and freezers, the energy label (see Figure 2.3) is graded into seven categories of efficiency; it is being extended to cover washing machines, dryers, dishwashers, ovens, water heaters, light sources and air-conditioning; other appliances will follow. The power of such labels was demonstrated during an early trial in Denmark that rapidly led to retailers withdrawing from sale the worst-performing appliances.

Labelling schemes are also becoming important driving forces in other parts of the world too, although once again they are far from static. For example, the criteria for the Japanese EcoMark – launched in 1989 – are being reviewed, as the standards were so low that a vast number of products qualified, thus making the label virtually meaningless. In the USA, labelling is generally being left to independent certification bodies, of which Scientific Certification Systems (SCS) is the oldest and largest dealing with environmental claims. SCS has certified products as varied as showerheads, paints, floor tiling and garden hoses, criteria including recycled content, biodegradability, and no smog-producing ingredients. SCS does not limit its approval schemes to products: it has, for example, approved as 'well-managed' a one million acre timber forest in Maine.

Figure 2.3 **EU energy label**

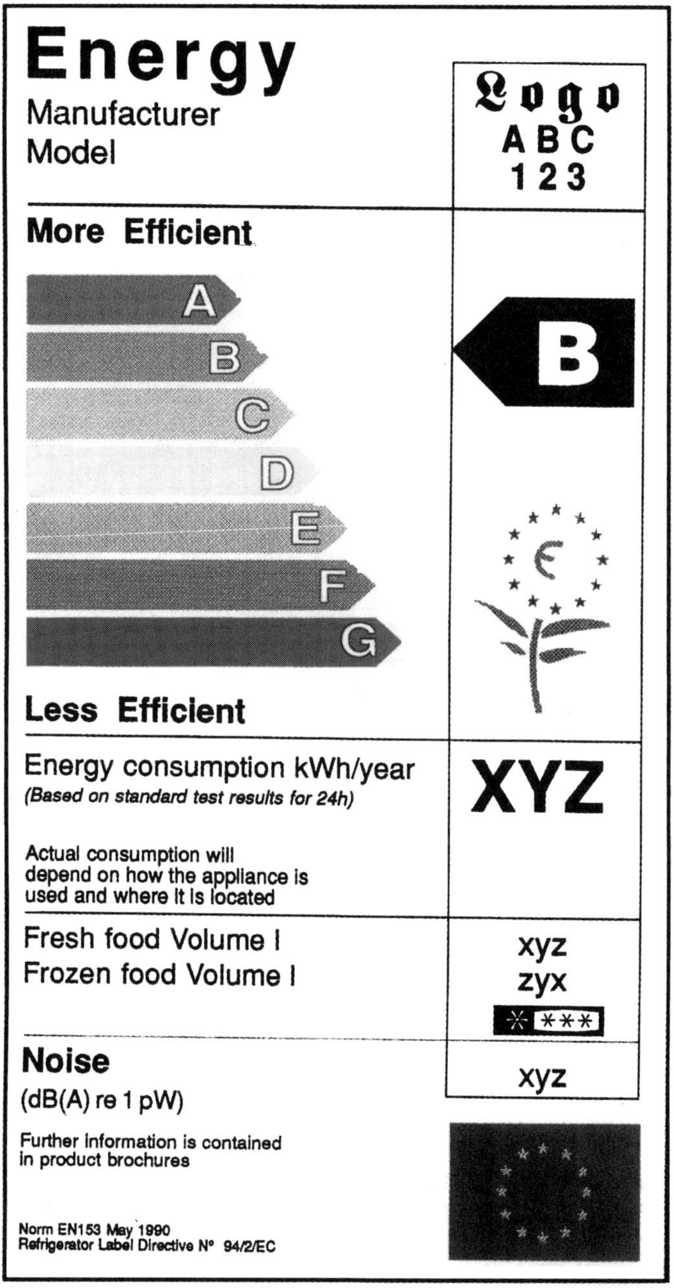

Energy

Manufacturer
Model

𝕷𝖔𝖌𝖔
A B C
1 2 3

More Efficient

B

Less Efficient

| Energy consumption kWh/year *(Based on standard test results for 24h)* | **XYZ** |

Actual consumption will
depend on how the appliance is
used and where it is located

Fresh food Volume I	xyz
Frozen food Volume I	zyx
	✳ ✳✳✳

Noise
(dB(A) re 1 pW)

xyz

Further information is contained
in product brochures

Norm EN153 May 1990
Refrigerator Label Directive N° 94/2/EC

The European Union energy rating label is becoming mandatory on products such as refrigerators and freezers. It is an information label, indicating into which of seven categories of efficiency the product falls and providing information about annual running costs and noise levels.

Environmental reporting

The voluntary labelling of the environmental performance of products is being paralleled by the voluntary provision of environmental information about companies as a whole. And once again the indications are that commercial pressures will soon begin to make such environmental reporting essential for many businesses, even if in theory it is voluntary. The UK government's Advisory Committee on Business and the Environment (ACBE) considers that there is a clear case for businesses reporting on their environmental performance.

> It will become increasingly difficult to operate without demonstrating due regard to environmental liabilities ... Given that the institutional investment community's primary concern and duty is to the value of its investments, it will grow increasingly sensitive to the cost implications of environmental performance ... lenders and insurers are already seeking further information on potential environmental opportunities and liabilities ... corporate customers are becoming increasingly interested in environmental information.[5]

The Institute of Chartered Accountants agrees. In the report *Business, Accountancy and the Environment,* published in 1992, the Institute suggested how environmental performance could be incorporated into business reporting. Ian Plaistowe, the Institute's President, said 'Good environmental practice is an integral part of good business practice and should permeate all aspects of the business.'[6]

BS 7750 Environmental Management Systems

Two initiatives are now formalising the way in which companies report their environmental performance. British Standard 7750

Environmental Management Systems is the environmental counterpart of the well-established BS 5750 on quality management. Just as BS 5750 has become a prerequisite for any company wanting to do business with major private and public organisations, so BS 7750 is likely to become essential too. The Environmental Management Standard does not set environmental targets as such but ensures that a company sets up its management structure in a way that ensures that all the relevant issues are taken into account; the Standard deals with management systems for everything from a company's products to the way it operates its sites and buildings.

EU Ecomanagement and Audit Scheme

The second initiative is the European Union's Ecomanagement and Audit Scheme (EMAS). Companies seeking to register under this scheme must have a company policy on the environment and a quantified programme and targets for the site in question. The programme and targets are set by the company but must cover all significant environmental impacts both directly for internal operations and indirectly elsewhere; regular audits are required, as is public disclosure of information on environmental performance in an annual report. The reliability and coverage of the information in these public statements must be checked by an independent third party. Unlike the British Standard scheme, the EU scheme calls for a ratcheting up of performance over time, thus providing an incentive for the development of more environmentally friendly products and processes. The EU scheme was launched in the UK in 1995 and is targeted in the first phase at industrial sites.

Box 2.4 EU Ecomanagement and Audit Scheme (EMAS)

The basic requirements for EMAS are:
- A company environmental policy which provides compliance with existing legislation and a commitment to reasonable, continuous improvement.
- An environmental review covering all aspects of the site(s).
- An environmental programme setting out quantified objectives for each site.
- An environmental management system which can be the company's own or a recognised standard such as BS 7750.
- An environmental audit cycle to provide regular information on the progress of the programme.
- A public environmental statement of progress issued after each audit.
- Validation of compliance by an independent verifier.

Box 2.5 International environmental management standards

The International Standards Organisation is developing standards for a comprehensive environmental management system. The standards will cover six areas:
- Environmental management systems, based on the EU Ecomanagement and Audit Scheme (EMAS) and BS 7750.
- Environmental auditing (which will also relate to EMAS).
- Environmental labelling, which will probably cover three types: a product label indicating approval to set standards, such as the Ecolabel; a self-declaration label (e.g. 'no CFCs'); and an information label akin to nutrition labels on food.
- Environmental performance and review: with no existing standards to work on, the ISO subcommittee is examining management systems for people; operational systems for processes and hardware; and environmental systems covering impacts at local, regional and global levels.
- Lifecycle assessment.
- Terms and definitions (aimed at ensuring international compatibility in key languages).

International standards

An International Standard is also under development. ISO 14000 seems likely to be less prescriptive than either BS 7750 or EMAS and may be especially suitable to the more regulatory approach favoured in the USA; the final standard is due to be published in

1996. Already, ISO 9000 – the international quality standard based on BS 5750 – has been extended to include health, safety and environmental issues as being a part of quality.

All of these schemes demand a company-wide strategy to deal with environmental issues – including product development programmes. Companies that have embraced Total Quality Management (TQM) will recognise that the approaches being recommended for dealing with environmental concerns do not merely parallel TQM but can in practice be incorporated as a natural extension of TQM.

The influence that voluntary schemes of product labelling and company auditing will have depend, of course, on how much consequence is placed on environmental issues by those who have a direct influence on business success.

Fiscal pressures

Another potential driving force for more environmentally-aware product development is the attitude of investors. But anyone looking for a clear direction from the financial community on environmental issues will be disappointed, for the picture is complex. A survey carried out by NOP at the end of 1994 on behalf of Business in the Environment found that most City analysts in the UK would opt for a firm with a poor environmental record but better trading results. But six out of ten said that Green issues had affected their assessment of companies and 69 per cent were concerned about the financial costs of environmental liabilities. Incidentally, 58 per cent of the 85 analysts in 28 sectors interviewed considered themselves well-informed on Green issues; but, perhaps surprisingly, all the engineering analysts said they had little or no Green knowledge.[7]

A different picture is given by the success of those financial institutions that specifically take an ethical stance that includes refusing to do business with companies associated with notable environmental damage. Their success is measured both by a faster than average rate of growth and, generally, by excellent profitability. For example, the Co-op Bank announced in 1992 that it would no longer do business with organisations involved in unethical enterprises: within a year, its customer base had increased by 13 per cent (treble the normal growth rate) and profits had nearly doubled.

There are other indications of the willingness of private investors to back environmental projects. For example, a British bank – Mercury Provident – linked with the Dutch Triodosbank to set up a special investment fund dedicated entirely to renewable energy, mostly small wind farms. Within two months of its launch in 1995, it attracted £500,000 in subscriptions from the public.

Insurance companies may be more ready to bring pressure on companies that ignore environmental issues, for they are becoming especially concerned about the long-term legal

---

Box 2.6 Insurers invest in Green technologies

The insurance industry has become so concerned about the huge claims that may arise from damage caused by global warming that it is taking the lead in encouraging technologies that will help head-off disaster. For example, American Re, a major US reinsurance company, has set up a subsidiary specifically to help develop environmentally-friendly technologies and is actively seeking to invest in solar power companies.

In the UK, a report prepared for the three leading insurance institutions recommended that the insurance industry should adopt a Green investment policy to combat global warming. The report, written in 1995, urged the industry to switch its investment in fossil fuel generators – worth more than £60 billion world-wide – into alternative energy provision.

liabilities for environmental damage. While they are primarily worried about the costs of clearing up major pollution incidents and contaminated land, their attention is also beginning to focus on product liability. After all, if the manufacturers of cigarettes can be sued for the long-term damage to health caused by smoking, it is not too difficult to foresee the day when vehicle manufacturers are sued for the damage that pollution causes to health and buildings: although the damage could not be pinned on a specific vehicle, the comparatively small number of manufacturers involved may well present the lawyers with a case to argue.

Green taxes

Of more immediate effect are the fiscal incentives being increasingly given by governments to promote environmental improvement. The UK government, for example, reduced the duty on unleaded petrol and thus provided an effective boost to persuade motorists to switch from leaded fuel. More recently, the government has announced that it is to impose a new tax on waste dumped in landfill sites as a means of encouraging recycling and waste minimisation.

Elsewhere, actions range from the German government's promotion of cleaner diesel cars by giving a £190 reduction in road tax for those emitting 0.08 grams or less of soot per cubic metre compared with the EU limit of 0.14 grams to the returnable deposit scheme initiated by the Dutch government in 1990 for a range of consumer goods to encourage recycling.

Incentives from the private sector

Financial incentives to encourage less environmentally damaging products can come from commercial sources too. One example was a group of American power companies that offered a prize to the manufacturer of the first refrigerator designed to use at least 25 per cent less electricity than required by current standards and that also used no CFCs. The prize for the winner – Whirlpool – was not just enormous publicity but also $30 million, paid out as a $10 bonus on each fridge sold.

For the future, probably the most significant financial influence on product design will concern energy. There seems little doubt that growing concern about the damaging effects of global warming and climate change will force governments to take drastic action to curb emissions from fossil fuels and encourage energy efficiency. While the European Union's energy tax proposals – which were heading towards a tax that could have increased fuel bills by around the equivalent of $10 a barrel of oil – collapsed in 1994, a number of countries have indicated that they may go ahead on their own. The UK government has itself already made one such move, having committed itself to raising petrol prices by at least 5 per cent in real terms every year for the foreseeable future. Few observers doubt that higher energy prices will be a major feature of future government and international environmental strategies.

The next chapter looks in more detail about the opportunities for business to profit from environmentally-sensitive product development.

3 Opportunities and benefits

■ Introduction ■ Commercial chaining ■ New markets
■ Green efficiency ■ The payback ■ The changing
challenge

Introduction

Early measures to tackle the environmental challenge
concentrated on end-of-pipe solutions, cleaning up pollution that
already existed. Product design was not an issue. That position
has now changed dramatically: for example, the UK government,
in its 1994 report, *Sustainable Development: the UK Strategy*, accepted
that the emphasis in the UK on the waste end of the lifecycle may
have been misguided. 'Effective waste minimisation is not just a
question of reducing unwanted outputs from the manufacturing
processes. It also involves producing ... longer lasting products',
said the report.

Governments in the Netherlands, Sweden and France are also
putting greater emphasis on environmentally-conscious product
development. For instance, during the preparation of the
regulation on waste from electronic products in Germany, the
Ministry of the Environment expressed its specific interest in the
process of product development and product design. This
emphasis on product design in the electronics industry is
reflected in the plans – referred to in the last chapter – of the UK
Industry Council for Electronic Equipment Recycling for a levy

***Box 3.1* Criteria for environmentally-sensitive product design**

There is broad international agreement about the basic criteria that a product has to meet to minimise environmental damage. Criteria include:
- Avoidance of materials that are toxic or that involve substantial environmental damage in their extraction or processing.
- Efficient use of materials, energy and other resources in manufacture and use.
- Encourage the user to minimise environmental damage when using the product.
- Facilitate long life by simplifying repair and upgrading.
- Expedite re-use and recycling.

on all new products to pay for recycling.' Over the longer term, any levies must reflect and reward environmental good practice in specific products, that is, a product which has been designed to minimise impact on the environment throughout its life should carry a lower levy', says ICER.

In the Netherlands, the government has a specific policy on products and the environment, the primary object of which is 'to bring about a situation whereby all market actors – producers, traders and consumers – are involved in an ongoing effort to reduce the impact which products have upon the environment'.[1]

In the United States, John H. Gibbons, the Director of the powerful Congressional Office of Technology Assessment, also sees product development as crucial. In 1992 he stated:

> Product design is an important environmental focal point, because design decisions directly and indirectly determine levels of resource use and the composition of waste streams ... Because product design encompasses the most crucial decision making activities of companies, the consideration of environmental objectives by designers could have important competitive implications. Market opportunities for environmentally sensitive goods and services are expanding.[2]

Good for business

The view that product innovation driven by environmental factors can be good for business is shared by business leaders. Jonathan Williams, of the UK Group for Environmental Manufacturing, has pointed out that

> the key environmental objectives of innovation include: elimination of hazardous or proscribed substances from products and manufacturing processes; improved resource efficiency throughout the product's life, with possible benefits from increased product durability; minimum waste generation in manufacture, use and end-of-life treatment; and facilitation of end-of-life treatment to maximise residual value, which will usually involve maximising the marketability of reclaimed resources. The last three of these objectives can also deliver economic benefit to the manufacturer and user.[3]

One of the earliest examples of the commercial benefits to be gained from a positive approach to environmental product development came in response to the US Clean Air Act of the 1970s aimed at reducing pollution problems caused by motor vehicle emissions. The new standards produced two markedly different responses from competing American and Japanese automobile manufacturers. The US car manufacturers saw environmental considerations as being subsidiary to the manufacturing process and sought an end-of-pipe solution through the introduction of catalytic converters into the exhaust system. In contrast, the Japanese – operating within an organisational culture and structure more conducive to change – integrated pollution measures into their production process and obtained improvements through engine redesign. This not only gave them an advantage in meeting emission standards but also improved their engine efficiency. With the onset of the oil crisis, this competitive advantage was compounded as the market for high efficiency engines increased; this led directly to the current dominance of Japanese motor manufacturers in many world markets.

Commercial chaining

While Green buying pressures from the general public are in their infancy, the pressures from the commercial world for more environmentally-sensitive products is already well-established. Leading the demand are organisations that, for one reason or another, have a special interest in environmental issues: retailers – especially the large supermarket chains – are extremely sensitive to public pressure as they are the first to feel any backlash from an environmental scandal; chemical companies, too, are in the front-line of environmental consideration and therefore seek to demonstrate their consideration for the environment throughout their operations; architects are increasingly becoming Green specifiers as worries about sick building syndrome and the energy efficiency of buildings increase; and government organisations want to be seen to be leading in cleaning up the environment.

Organisations such as B&Q are not confining their environmental policies to their own operations: they are seeking to ensure that their suppliers have a sound environmental record as well. This chaining of environmental responsibility echoes the revolution that has forced companies to adopt formal quality management standards in recent years and the demand for both manufacturing and service companies to prove their environmental credentials to their commercial customers is growing rapidly.

One retailer that has demonstrated the power of chaining

Box 3.2 B&Q gets tough on suppliers

The major UK DIY store group B&Q has set up a Supplier Environmental Audit (SEA) system to gather information about its suppliers, who are then graded on a six-point scale, the top grade requiring a demonstration of environmental excellence, including a well-documented and systematic programme backed by innovative responses to environmental issues.

At the beginning of 1994, fewer than 60 per cent of B&Q's suppliers were at a grade C or above. To force progress, the B&Q Board set tight deadlines. All suppliers were given less than a year to achieve grade C or face losing their B&Q business (grade C required a written policy identifying key issues associated with products and a firm commitment to addressing them). The company offered considerable support to assist its suppliers in meeting its requirements. By November 1994, 94 per cent of suppliers had achieved grade C, ten had been delisted, and eight had been granted a time extension.

B&Q claims that SEA has achieved four goals: compliance with the company's corporate policy; a written commitment to improvement from all suppliers; a body of information on the environmental impacts of all B&Q products; and a huge increase in understanding among suppliers.

B&Q has merged its environmental and quality policies, the ultimate aim being to ensure that no product will be stocked unless it has met both environmental and quality standards. 'Our environmental programme has not just brought direct cost benefits', commented Jim Hodkinson, B&Q's Chairman and Chief Executive. 'Through our environmental policy we have been recognised as a responsible retailer and there is no doubt that our corporate image has benefited.'

---

environmental responsibility is the major do-it-yourself company B&Q. It has insisted that all of its suppliers complete a detailed questionnaire about their environmental performance (see Box 3.2) and has shown no hesitation in acting on the results. For example, B&Q dropped Fisons as a peat supplier after that company failed to give assurances on its environmental performance; that hurt, for B&Q sells 40 per cent of all garden peat supplied in the UK. B&Q has since developed its environmental policy into a far-reaching strategy that is changing the attitudes of many manufacturers' suppliers: further examples from B&Q's experience are given later in this book.

Packaging and paper has been in the forefront of public

environmental attention and this has attracted close attention from many companies. For instance, Boots has carried out an audit of the packaging for all its 50,000 lines and established a baseline for retail, display and transit packaging. Since 1993, all new Boots brand specifications have required suppliers to provide information on the packaging material used, including such details as recycled content, re-use rate and the weights of all packaging and components. Boots claims that the programme has saved money, waste and pollution.

Boots is one of the companies – along with organisations such as HMSO and Marks & Spencer – that have formed the Paper Users' Environmental Forum. The Forum has produced a Paper Buyer's Environmental Checklist requiring answers to three questions before paper is purchased: has the paper an independent environmental endorsement?; what proportion is virgin or recycled fibre?; and what process was used to whiten the paper?

All kinds of product

Another major organisation that is systematically scrutinising the environmental record of its suppliers is the National Westminster Bank. NatWest has developed a consistent approach for its purchasing units to prioritise suppliers, products and services for attention regarding environmental impact and intends to make environmental appraisal an integral part of supplier selection. With more than 20,000 suppliers, the multiplier effect of such chaining is obvious.

Many local authorities, too, are adopting environmental purchasing policies, providing substantial market opportunities for everything from water-efficient toilets and pollution-free laser printers to sophisticated heat recovery systems for swimming

> **Box 3.3** Pentel goes solvent-free
>
> Marker pens usually contain solvents such as toluene and xylene that are both toxic and are sometimes associated with solvent abuse. Pentel has developed an alternative range that uses an alcohol-based ink that is permanent on most surfaces. The cap of the pen has an air-flow feature that prevents suffocation if it is swallowed.

pools and fuel-efficient vehicles.

Environmental chaining is rapidly spreading into other commercial areas. For example, the UK Civil Aviation Authority now includes energy efficiency in all its specifications for radio and radar equipment. Again, the furniture industry is not immune: Carson Office Furniture Systems has reported that it is under growing pressure to provide evidence of environmental, health and safety issues. 'If you are dealing with government departments, for example, you have to have BS 5750 or ISO 9000 to get on the tender list in the first place. The same thing is starting to apply for environmental standards', said the company's quality and environment manager in 1995.

The chaining effect is being felt all over the world. 'Customers, especially sophisticated customers, are demanding environmentally appropriate products. They do not know how to define them yet – neither do we – but the demand is there. Markets are beginning to be defined by environmental considerations', commented the Research Vice-President of the giant American communications company AT&T at a conference in 1994. This view was repeated by the Marketing Programmes Manager of the $2 billion information products company Lexmark International: 'Our corporate customers give significant weight to the environment. We rarely see an invitation to tender without some mention of environmental management. Potential customers want to be fully confident that we are a responsible company.'

Smaller companies

Small companies are feeling the chaining pressures too. The survey of small firms carried out in 1994 by the British Chambers of Commerce and referred to in Chapter 2 found that 18 per cent had experienced pressure from customers to improve environmental performance, mostly with regard to materials or the nature of the product; 15 per cent of the small companies surveyed had themselves placed pressure on suppliers to improve their environmental performance.

British Standard 7750 *Environmental Management Systems* is a significant driving force for chaining, as it requires a company to put in place procedures to check on the major environmental impacts of supplier companies. More importantly, BS 7750 (along with the European Union's Ecomanagement and Audit Scheme) provides a relatively simple means for companies to be assured that their suppliers are behaving in an environmentally responsible manner.

Box 3.4 Aquablast cleans cleaning

Cleaning off paint and rust can be dangerous and environmentally-unfriendly using traditional methods of grit-blasting, chemical cleaning or wire-brushing. Aquablast Ltd has developed an alternative using ultra-high pressure water instead, thus avoiding the need to dispose of abrasives or chemicals or the risk of these damaging equipment on board ships or oil-rigs or in industrial situations. The Aquablast system uses twin hydraulic intensifiers to create a water pressure as high as 60,000 psi, enough to easily clean off rust or thick layers of paint or other coatings from steel or other surfaces. The system is especially attractive to users in industries such as oil and chemicals, where environmental issues are high on the agenda.

In some fields, more specific environmental performance criteria are being demanded from suppliers. For example, an energy efficiency accreditation scheme was launched in the UK in 1994. This may itself be required as part of BS 7750 in future.

The message for business is clear: no company is likely to remain isolated from environmental pressures for much longer. Supplier chaining is rapidly becoming all-embracing; consumer demand for Greener products is growing; fiscal penalties and incentives to reduce environmental impacts are beginning to bite; and the national and international regulation of environmentally damaging activities is becoming tougher.

This is not bad news for business. As the International Chamber of Commerce said in its *Business Charter for Sustainable Development* in 1991:

> Versatile, dynamic, responsive and profitable businesses are required as the driving force for sustainable economic development and for providing managerial, technical and financial resources to contribute to the resolution of environmental challenges. Market economies, characterised by entrepreneurial initiatives, are essential to achieving this. Business thus shares the view that there should be a common goal, not a conflict, between economic development and environmental protection, both now and for future generations.

The Charter recognises the key role of product development, calling for companies to develop and provide products or services that 'have no undue environmental impact and are safe in their intended use, that are efficient in their consumption of energy and natural resources, and that can be recycled, reused or disposed of safely'.

The remainder of this chapter looks in more detail at the commercial benefits to be gained from environmental product development, including the new markets created by environmental concerns, the inherent efficiency gains, and the longer-term opportunities for entrepreneurial businesses.

New markets

The most obvious businesses to benefit from the environmental revolution are those supplying equipment and services aimed directly at solving pollution problems. These range from monitoring equipment and waste treatment plants to catalytic converters for cars and filtration equipment for power station chimneys. In 1993, the OECD valued the global market for environmental technology at $200 billion and forecast that it would reach $300 billion by 2000.

Environmental forces are generating entirely new industries, especially in the energy field. Solar cells – once little more than a gimmick in calculators – are rapidly becoming ubiquitous not just as a power source for equipment is areas remote from a mains supply but as a replacement for conventional generating capacity. For example, buildings in many parts of the world are beginning to feature solar cells as a partial source of their electrical needs. Wind turbines are now well-established as commercial Green power sources. Heat pumps and other energy recovery systems are in increasing demand too. Opportunities for new consumer products have also appeared. One of the oddest was the provision of booths in Mexico City where people can breathe pure oxygen at a cost of $2 a minute, the demand for which was a direct result of that city's air pollution. Fears about pollution were also the original driving force for the introduction of bottled drinking water, now a multi-million pound world-wide industry. There are now Green mail order catalogues offering everything from recycled gift wrapping paper and rucksacks made from recycled fabric to a recycling can crusher and special bins for composting domestic waste. The Savaplug illustrated in Figure 3.1 is just one example of a number of novel devices aimed at improving the energy efficiency of existing products.

Rejuvenating old products

Environmental motivation is also providing opportunities to rejuvenate old products and to gain market advantage for those that are redesigned. The most obvious example of the former is the rebirth of re-usable nappies; these are being promoted as the Green alternative to disposables, which are now a major component of domestic waste, with 80 tonnes of disposable nappies thrown away every hour in the UK alone. An early instance of a company gaining a commercial advantage with a product redesigned to reduce its environmental impact was the German battery maker Varta. It launched its mercury-free battery in the UK at the end of 1988, stressing its Greenness with the clever marketing device of including some flower seeds in the pack. As a result, Varta's share of the UK market increased by 50 per cent within six months.

Another company that has learned the lesson that environmentally-inspired product development can reap substantial commercial benefits is the Swedish manufacturer Electrolux. It won a competition run by the Swedish Board for Industrial and Technical Development aimed at improving the efficiency of refrigeration appliances with a design that was around 60 per cent more efficient than existing models. The new product rapidly won orders for more than 10,000 units and

Figure 3.1 Savaplug cuts the costs of refrigeration

UK households spend around £1,000 million a year on electricity for fridges and freezers. The Savaplug has been designed to cut these costs and reduce pollution by up to 15 per cent. The Savaplug was developed under a UK government research and development programme and has since been manufactured and marketed successfully by Savawatt (UK) Ltd. The Savaplug replaces the ordinary electrical plug on the appliance and works by improving the control of the motor. (Savawatt UK Ltd.)

Electrolux subsequently developed further new models to meet the demand. This success was not confined to the Swedish market: the new models took 50 per cent of the company's share of the German market and were successful elsewhere too.

Some companies still see environmental pressures as being entirely negative, as restrictive and expensive. Such companies are missing major opportunities for profits and growth.

Green efficiency

The commercial benefits of environmentally-driven product development are not confined to the creation of new market opportunities, for there is an inherent link between environmentally-responsible design and efficiency. The prime objective of environmentally-conscious design is to use resources efficiently, thus minimising their use and avoiding waste. These objectives also lead to reduced costs for the manufacturer and the user.

The immense opportunities for such efficiency gains can be gauged by looking at the gross inefficiency of current economies. For instance, in the United States 10 tonnes of active material is extracted for each person every year, yet only 6 per cent of this is embodied into durable goods, the other 94 per cent being converted into waste within a few months of being extracted.

Later chapters will look in more detail at how designers can set about meeting the efficiency objectives that benefit both business

---

Box 3.5 **Oki designs more efficient printers**

The Oki range of computer printers uses LED technology in place of a laser to eliminate ozone production and also features a number of innovations to minimise the use of energy and other consumable resources. For example, the printers have separate toner and drum units, allowing each to be used for its maximum life without the compromise inherent in the usual combined unit. Unused toner is automatically recycled within the machine. Oki claims that users can save between £50 and £75 a year through these resource-efficient features.

Box 3.6 Marks & Spencer adopts minimum packaging policy

The major retailer Marks & Spencer has adopted a policy of using the absolute minimum amount of packaging necessary to perform its function. The policy is part of M&S's long-term strategy of minimising costs and is not driven primarily either by environmental factors or by growing public concern with overpackaging. 'Wherever there is an environmental benefit to be made, there is invariably a cost benefit', says Len Randall, the company's environmental manager. 'For instance, for many years our supply chain has delivered the majority of food products from farms and factories to retail outlets in returnable plastic trays which replaced one-trip cartons. The development has paid for itself several times over.'

---

and the environment. Here are just a few examples of the direct benefits gained by some manufacturers:

- The Japanese laser printer manufacturer Canon reduced the weight of material in a new toner cartridge by 70 per cent.

- British Alcan developed a re-usable delivery system for narrow, large diameter coils of heavy gauge aluminium foil for use in the car industry. Developed in co-operation with the Ford Motor Company, this cost £60,000 but saved the costs of temporary racking and avoided the waste of 2,000 tonnes a year of scrap wood, steel banding and plastic film.

- Skippingdale Paper Products Ltd has saved £195,000 a year on transport costs simply by reducing the volume of disposable nappy packs by almost 60 per cent.

- When Hoover designed a washing machine specifically to meet the criteria for the Ecolabelling scheme, it also bought new delivery lorries and ensured that these were designed to maximise the number of the new machines carried; loads were increased by 20 per cent, cutting both the capital cost of new vehicles and delivery costs.

- In the United States, a government-inspired Green Lights Program – aimed at improving the energy efficiency of lighting in businesses and homes – is expected to make annual energy savings of \$763 million by 1997 and also save 7 million tonnes of carbon dioxide a year.

The payback

A significant contribution to understanding the commercial benefits of investing in Green product development has been made by a study in the United Kingdom carried out by two researchers, Dr Robin Roy and Dr Stephen Potter, of the Open University's Design Innovation Group. Working with researchers from the University of Manchester Institute of Science and Technology, they had earlier carried out a study into the commercial results of investing in general engineering and industrial design projects. Roy and Potter have now used the same methodology to look specifically at the bottom-line results of investing in Green design.

The earlier research had shown that 89 per cent of general design projects that reach production make a profit. Almost a half pay back the total investment – including tooling and other costs – in less than a year. The research into design-for-the-environment projects suggests that such investments could bring even better rewards. Although only 16 companies have been examined so far in this new study, Potter and Roy found that, on average, Green design projects achieved a higher proportion of exports (25 per cent compared with 19 per cent) and a marginally higher gross profit margin (40 per cent compared with 37 per cent) than did the general projects. However, the cost of developing Green products was, on average, approximately double that for general projects. Despite this, payback was relatively rapid and sales growth impressive.[4]

Figure 3.2 **Boehringer halves manufacturing costs**

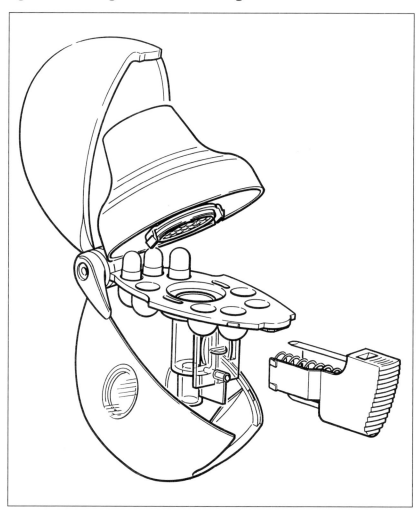

The 'HandiHaler' – designed by UK consultancy Kinneir Dufort for the German pharmaceutical group Boehringer – is used to treat asthma, a disease whose rapid growth is mostly due to increased pollution. The design team has delivered major advantages over earlier systems for delivering medication, the primary benefits coming from sealing the inhalation chamber in an airtight shell when not in use. This removes the need for a separate zip-up pouch, reducing material usage and playing a substantial part in reducing the unit manufacturing cost to half that of Boehringer's standard powdered drug inhaler. It also helps to make the device easy to use and compact. (Kinneir Dufort Design Ltd.)

Table 3.1 Green design criteria cited by companies

Criteria	Percentage of companies
Materials used in product	19
Pollution/waste from manufacture	16
Energy consumed in use	13
Environmental impacts of use	11
Potential for recycling	11
Pollution/waste in disposal	11
Energy consumed during manufacture	8
Design for re-use	5
Other	5

Note: Most companies mentioned several criteria
Source: Open University Design Innovation Group

The Open University study revealed a wide range of environmental considerations being taken into account in Green design projects (see Table 3.1). Nearly a fifth of the companies looked at environmental factors when selecting materials and components; pollution and waste in the manufacturing process was the next most mentioned factor, while energy performance, recycling potential, pollution from disposal and design for re-use were all considered by three or more of the sample companies.

Only one of the 16 companies covered by the survey thought that environmental performance was the single most important factor in its competitive edge; most attributed their success to overall quality, specification and value for money. 'The key message from our research is that an environmental perspective spurs companies into an approach to innovation and design that leads to efficient, high performance, profitable products', said Stephen Potter.

The following brief case histories are extracted from the survey information to illustrate the variety of commercial benefits identified.

Powering Green growth

Nitech was launched in 1981 to exploit a market boosted by European environmental legislation that demanded higher safety standards in hazardous areas. Its first product was the 'X-cell' high performance rechargeable battery with integral charger, which can replace 3,000 ordinary batteries and thus save 300 times its own cost as well as avoiding the disposal of 2.5 tonnes of throw-away batteries.

Nitech has gradually built up a range of torches and other products to exploit its battery innovation, concentrating on the demand for reliable, high-performance products for professional users who include the police, military and companies such as BT and British Airways. The company has a continuous product development policy and launched four products in 1994, including the world's first rechargeable portable electronic floodlight. Nitech's sales grew steadily during the recession of the early 1990s, from £1.12 million in 1990 to £1.75 million in 1993. It won the Exporter of the Year Award in 1992.

More from less

Trannon Furniture designs and makes high quality furniture from forest thinnings and coppiced wood, thus converting what is usually an underutilised material into a high value product. While the conservation benefits were a motivating factor for designer David Colwell, his business partner Roy Tam readily points out the commercial advantages: 'The material bends well, is straight-grained, and is stronger than timber from mature trees. Although there is greater wastage than mature timber, it costs less, so we are not paying a premium to go Green.' Trannon had to develop new techniques for bending and shaping thinnings, including looking at which woods can be shaped while still green and learning how to exploit the very special aesthetics of the materials. Launched at the end of 1991, sales reached £200,000 in 1994 with orders for such prestige buildings as the Science Museum in Birmingham and considerable interest from abroad.

Packaging savings

S.C. Johnson, one of the world's leading manufacturers of home care products, continues the caring traditions of its nineteenth century American founder. In 1990, the company set a series of environmental goals, including one that called for a 20 per cent reduction in the amount of virgin material as a ratio to the formula weight in its packaging by 1995. The UK company took a twin-track approach to meeting this target. Its first initiative was to develop a way of using 100 per cent recycled plastic for its 'Shake N' Vac' carpet and room freshener. It then turned to redesigning packs to minimise materials' use, an approach that has both environmental and economic benefits. As a result, the weight of paperboard used for 'Pottery' air freshener refill boxes has been cut by more than 20 per cent by eliminating some flaps; the 'Plug-in' box has also been redesigned, saving almost 50 tons of paperboard a year. By the end of 1992, the programme had cut the use of virgin material by 6.6 per cent compared with 1990. S.C. Johnson's European Consumer Products business achieved a 9 per cent virgin packaging reduction compared with 1990.

The changing challenge

New commercial opportunities arising from environmental pressures will unfold in the future. One of the first is likely to come from the use of new materials, especially natural materials. The Japanese government has recognised the potential and, in

1993, began a five year research project to develop easily recyclable materials and ways of increasing the use of natural materials.

There are already examples of products being made from renewable materials. For example, a Japanese company is manufacturing a bicycle made from paper combined with an epoxy resin to make it waterproof. Again, electric fencing is being made in the United States with posts milled from the Australian eucalyptus tree; this has the advantage that the wood does not conduct electricity and the fencing therefore requires no insulators. The £2 billion-a-year European market for the ubiquitous oil-derived foam 'peanuts' used for protecting fragile products during transport is under attack from Danish scientists who are experimenting with using Sesbania, an African legume-tree whose hollow stems can be chopped up and used as packaging.

A second change in the competitive climate seems likely to come from a switch in the way in which industry and consumers assess value for money. While some industries are well used to evaluating the lifetime costs of equipment – including such aspects as maintenance, energy, insurance and so on – this approach is rare among the general public and is not even general in the commercial world. For example, few companies appear to pay much attention to fuel efficiency when buying cars, despite the fact that fuel accounts for more than a quarter of the lifetime costs of a car.

Lifetime costing
Lifetime costing is such a low priority among consumers that a survey carried out by Coventry University found that, of nine manufacturers questioned, all were able to estimate their

manufacturing costs but only three had any idea of their customers' costs and only one could answer with any confidence.[5]

This situation is likely to change under the impetus of fiscal and other pressures to reduce resource use and cut waste. Energy labelling schemes will encourage consumers to start taking into account running costs when purchasing equipment such as refrigerators and cookers, while in the commercial world the economic advantages of basing buying decisions on whole-life costs rather than simply purchase price will force change.

Already some companies have turned the potential of lifetime costing to their own advantage. A good example is LTI Carbodies, the manufacturer of London's black taxis. In the late 1980s the company recognised that it needed to improve the quality of its product to avoid losing market share to other vehicles. LTI Carbodies decided to seek a competitive advantage by looking not just to reduce manufacturing costs but to reduce running costs too. The company was fortunate in having information on whole-life costs, as this was needed to assist sales and fare-setting. Typically, purchase costs accounted for around 22 per cent of whole-life costs, with servicing and fuel accounting for 64 per cent. By choosing a more fuel-efficient engine, some £6,000 was cut from the whole-life costs (around 14 per cent of the total cost of diesel used during the life of a vehicle); the new engine also enabled service intervals to be doubled, cutting another £4,700 from lifetime costs; attention to reliability of other components further reduced servicing costs by around another £6,000. Using these lifetime savings as a prime selling feature, the company was able to persuade buyers to pay a higher purchase price for the new taxi on the basis that, in the long run, they would save a significant amount of money. LTI Carbodies recovered its investment in the new design in just 18 months.[6]

Reducing consumption

In the long run, perhaps the most fundamental entrepreneurial challenge will come from the need to reduce overall consumption. This, of course, is often seen as the great threat to business. But it could also be an opportunity.

A report published by the Netherlands government has suggested that 'It may well be that the attainment of sustainable development will also require reductions in the quantity of products consumed and changes in our lifestyles. As incomes rise, consumption – or the satisfaction of demand – will have to be shifted towards non-material goods and the better and more efficient use of products. Such a shift need not involve any reduction in the quality of life.'[7]

Such a shift would also present at least two opportunities for companies with sound product development strategies. The first, of course, is the opportunity to develop the long-life products needed to achieve the aim of relaxing the link between the quality of life and the numbers of products purchased. As long ago as the 1970s, the car maker Porsche had carried out a study into the feasibility of producing cars that would last for between 18 and 25 years; this concluded that such a long-life car would lead to a saving of 55 per cent in the use of resources. More recently, the University of Wuppertal Institute in Germany has designed a hybrid cool storage facility that combines the traditional kitchen cupboard and refrigerator function and that has been designed to last as long as the house into which it is built (see Figure 3.3).

The second opportunity from such a shift seems likely to be for companies to switch from being a provider of products to being a provider of services. Thus a heating appliance manufacturer might evolve into a provider of warmth, being paid for the service

Figure 3.3 **Long-life refrigeration**

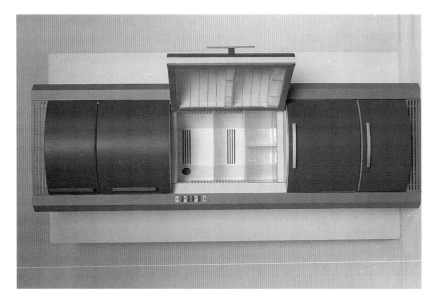

The FRIA cooling system designed by Ursula Tischner at the Wuppertal Institute should outlive ten conventional refrigerators, thus making a net saving of around 80 per cent in materials. Designed for easy repair and incorporating the facility to change the handles and front panels to match new kitchen furniture, the FRIA utilises cold air from outside to reduce energy costs in winter, giving a net energy saving of around half compared with a conventional refrigerator. (Ursula Tischer/Wuppertal Institute.)

rather than the product. This, too, has important implications for product developers: a company selling a service that uses a product is far more interested in the lifetime costs than in the initial cost and this will place a premium on such attributes as reliability, repairability and upgradability. Such matters are dealt with more fully in later chapters.

John McConnell, a senior partner in the leading UK design consultancy Pentagram, has brought together the commercial and ethical arguments for environmental design. 'There are three degrees of ethical self-expression', he says. 'The first is to make a virtue out of necessity. If the requirements of environmental or social legislation must be met anyway, why not make a big deal of it? The second is to anticipate higher ethical standards and meet or exceed them in advance – then use this to competitive advantage. The third degree is to raise the standard of ethical practice for moral self-esteem rather than commercial gain.' The evidence is that, in the long term and with an innovative approach to design and to business, what is good for the environment is generally good for business.

Incremental or radical?

In the next two chapters I look in detail at what is involved in developing more environmentally-responsible products. But it may be helpful to first discuss the choice between incremental improvement and a radical approach. The US Congress Office of Technology Assessment (OTA) has set two goals for Green design: waste prevention and better materials management. Within these objectives, the OTA focuses on eight detailed areas for analysis ranging from the minimisation of the use of resources to the extension of service life (see Table 3.2). While these are entirely laudable and should form the basis for any comprehensive approach to environmentally-aware product

Table 3.2 The dual goals of Green design

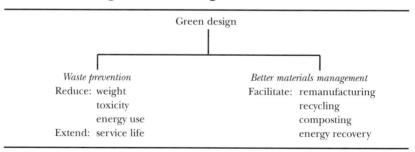

Source: US Congress Office of Technology Assessment

development, these goals do imply an incremental approach, examining and improving in detail the environmental performance of an existing broad product solution.

While this approach is appropriate for most circumstances and is reflected in most of the recommendations made later in this book, I should perhaps point out that it can lead to a blind alley, away from a radical and better solution. Many environmentalists argue that the first question to be asked is 'Does nature have a natural way of achieving the objective?'; if so, it is likely that this ecological approach will provide the basis for the best solution.

One example quoted by Stefan Bartha of the International Association of Ecological Design in Sweden is the problem of fouling organisms that attach themselves to the cooling systems of ships, power plants and factories that use seawater for cooling. The usual solution to the problem is to use a dosing pump to inject a poison into the system to kill the organisms. But Bartha points out that the larvae that cause the fouling are scarcely 0.5 mm in size and cannot attach themselves to the piping if the water flow exceeds 1 metre a second. So the ecological solution would be to design systems where the water flow is maintained at 1 metre a second, which presents no design difficulties as piping materials can withstand flows at least three times this speed.

Another point worth making is that what constitutes environmentally-responsible design depends on the product and the way it is used. It is affected by such factors as the length of product life (which is influenced both by the direct qualities of the product – durability and so on – and indirect factors such as fashionability) and the local conditions under which the product is to be used and disposed.

Improving product performance

There is sometimes a fear among designers and consumers that environmental considerations will undermine performance. This certainly appeared to be the case with some so-called Green detergents in the early eco-enthusiasm days. In reality, Green issues should put even greater emphasis on performance, for a product that performs inadequately will benefit neither the consumer nor the environment as it will rapidly be thrown away and replaced by one that performs properly.

In practice, environmentally-driven design should force product developers to raise questions that lead to improved performance, especially in terms of value-for-money and whole-life cost. For example, the medical world has long assumed that hygiene is best served by the use of disposable equipment, although this can be more expensive than sterilising equipment for re-use. Concerned about the environmental consequences of the growth in medical waste, Franz Daschner, Professor of Epidemiology at the University of Freiburg in Germany, carried out a control study involving the use of disposable catheters compared with re-usable ones disinfected with heat treatment. He found no difference in infection rates and warned that millions of pounds were being wasted in hospitals on disposable equipment that polluted the environment.

One worrying feature of some current approaches to environmental design is the undue emphasis placed by some designers and manufacturers – as well as by the public – on recycling as the prime tool to guide manufacturing on to the path of sustainability. Recycling has its place, but is relatively low down the priorities needed to achieve sustainable development. As the UK House of Commons Environment Committee warned in its 1994 report on recycling:

The danger, though, in our quest to use what can be used again in whatever form, is that a counter-culture develops of recycling for its own sake, no matter what the cost is in energy or money ... We are convinced of the fundamental preferability of waste reduction at source. Re-use and recovery (of both energy and materials) are the next best options. Disposal may sometimes be necessary but should be an option of last resort.

To summarise this chapter, there are clear and well-proven commercial benefits to be won from developing products that offer environmental advantages. But these benefits can only be maximised in the long term if the design team asks radical questions about the role of the product and examines alternative ways of delivering the service needed by the consumer.

4 The design considerations: materials and manufacturing

■ Introduction ■ Materials ■ Manufacturing

Introduction

This chapter and the one that follows examine the environmental implications for designers of each stage of a product's life, as I believe that this approach best illustrates the detailed considerations relevant to product development. For the sake of clarity, I have split product life into two, the first – dealt with in this chapter – being the making of the product and covering the choice of materials and the manufacturing aspects, with the second – considered in Chapter 5 – being use and end-of-life, including such aspects as durability, upgrading and recycling.

Materials

The life of a product begins with the acquisition of materials. For the design team, the choice of materials is far from simple. While design almost always involves trading-off one factor against another, nowhere is this more apparent than in making choices between materials in terms of their environmental impact. For example, choosing galvanised steel inhibits rust and can therefore extend the life of a product; but it also inhibits recycling. An apparently simple product such as a crisp packet can present complex choices: a pack consisting of layers of polypropylene and metallised aluminium can minimise weight and keep the contents fresh – thus providing waste prevention benefits – but such a pack is also difficult to recycle because of the mix of materials.

Information

There is also a major information problem. It has been estimated that some 160,000 chemicals have been synthesised, of which around 10,000 are in use; each has its own environmental footprint. To complicate matters further, the environmental impact of a particular material may vary wildly depending on its source. Recycled aluminium, for example, is many times less damaging than virgin aluminium: its production consumes only 5 per cent of the power needed to produce the virgin material and avoids the damage caused by the extraction of bauxite, some 20 per cent of which is mined and processed in areas of rainforest. But this is of little interest to most designers, as they are unlikely to have any control over the source of the material and in performance terms the two are virtually indistinguishable (there are exceptions: some reclaimed aluminium contains impurities that make it unsuitable for the wrought alloys used, for example, in structural car components).

Nevertheless, there is much that the design team can do in the choice and use of materials to minimise environmental impact. Methods of assessing environmental impact – especially the use of lifecycle analysis techniques – are discussed more fully in Chapter 6; here, it is only necessary to say that sufficient information about the environmental impacts of many materials is available in ways that can provide enough guidance to be of use in the design process. Table 4.1 shows as an example the comparative impacts of using two different plastics for the manufacture of a diskette

Table 4.1 Environmental profile of a diskette box

	HDPE	HIPS
Weight	83 g	83 g
Energy requirement	6.7 MJ	8.8 MJ
CO_2	102 g	174 g
CO	82.4 mg	157 mg
HCl	4.12 mg	4.12 mg
HF	0.08 mg	0.16 mg
Metals (water use)	25 mg	91 mg
NOx	910 mg	2,760 mg
SOx	0.6 mg	3.4 mg
Toxic chemicals	3.3 mg	0.08 mg

Source: Association of Plastics Manufacturers in Europe

Table 4.2 Amount of post-use scrap recycled as a percentage of consumption and energy saved through recycling

	Estimated home consumption (thousand tonnes)	Scrap (percentage)	Energy saved through recycling (percentage)
Ferrous metal	13,420	45	74
Aluminium	645	39	95
Copper	391	45	60–96
Lead	302	64	77
Zinc	237	21	61

Sources: Department of the Environment (1994) *Digest of Environmental Protection and Water Statistics*, London: HMSO; New Economics Foundation (1994) *Beyond Recycling*, London: NEF

box; Table 4.2 indicates the energy savings made by using recycled metals.

Where companies can influence the sources of materials, efforts should be made to seek supplies from those that are least environmentally damaging. Timber, for instance, can come from sustainable sources where it is grown on a farmed basis or it can come from suppliers who leave behind an ecological disaster. Although some timber growers and importers are endeavouring to set up reliable labelling schemes for timber from sustainable sources, at the time of writing almost all tropical hardwoods are suspect. Under these circumstances, designers are best advised to find alternatives and replace hardwoods such as mahogany and rosewood with either softwoods or temperate hardwoods. Again, most cotton is grown with heavy uses of chemicals which require substantial energy inputs to manufacture and which damage local ecosystems; but organic cotton – grown without pesticides, defoliants or artificial fertilisers – is becoming available and is being specified by some clothing manufacturers. Textiles generally are likely to come under close scrutiny in the near future due to the considerable quantities of heavy metals and toxins they contain – in some cases the quantities are so high that a lorry load of clothes should be treated as hazardous according to American EPA rules

Switching to renewable sources

Some products – furniture, for instance (see Figure 4.1 for an example) – have traditionally been manufactured from renewable materials. In future, the use of renewables is likely to extend as scientists discover new ways of manufacturing materials to replace those from non-renewable sources. For example, nylon is conventionally produced from benzene, a non-renewable and toxic fossil fuel; the process is energy intensive and produces around 10 per cent of all the nitrous oxide discharged into the atmosphere. An alternative is on the way: two scientists at Purdue University in the United States have found a method to biologically convert cellulose – available in large quantities as straw and other agricultural waste – to the adipic acid that is required for the manufacture of nylon.

Pressures for more environmentally sustainable processes are encouraging a switch to renewable resources in many areas. Oilseeds of various kinds can be a source for plastics; soya beans are

Figure 4.1 Seating system creates less waste

The Kin-der-Link school seating system won an IDEA design award in the United States in 1994 for its imaginative design which encourages creative uses by the children. The bent plywood stools can be interlinked in almost any shape, flexibility being provided by the linking mechanism, which entails slotting one leg into one of a choice of three holes. The plywood has a maple facing over a sweetgum core, both replenishable and biodegradable. Rotary cutting is used to minimise waste: 93 per cent of the original material ends up in the furniture, opposed to less than two-thirds if solid wood was to be used. A water-based acrylic/polyurethane finish minimises pollution risk. (Skools Inc.)

being used for paints, glues and printing inks; and special maize hybrids are being bred for industrial uses. One example is amylomaize, which has chemical properties that enable it to be used in films and clothing. Again, wheat may soon be an important source of industrial materials, its uses ranging from plastic bags to a replacement for stone aggregate in building blocks.

From the product developer's point of view there will in many cases be no difference in performance terms between a material from a renewable source and one from a finite source. So the choice will not affect the design specification. This is not so true of another source of Green materials, those recovered through recycling. In particular, plastics tend to degrade when recycled, especially when the material is recovered from post-consumer waste. This does not mean that they should not be used, only that great care should be taken to ensure that when they are used the necessary specification can be met consistently by the recycler (see Figure 4.2 for an example of a successful product manufactured from recycled plastics).

Growth in recycled materials

One sure way of achieving this is to plan the cascade of plastics materials through a chain of appropriate uses. For example, the electronics company Digital Equipment has arranged for the housings of its old computers in the United States to be recycled by GE Plastics, the resulting material then being manufactured into roof tiles by Nailite for use on McDonalds fast food restaurants. In the UK, the plastics housewares manufacturer Plysu has made an arrangement with a nearby local authority to

Figure 4.2 **Sitting on milk jugs**

The Petoskey Polysite bench has been designed by the American consultancy Becket and Raeder to use HDPE derived from discarded milk jugs. The frame is steel. (Becket and Raeder.)

take plastics waste, which it then recycles into compost bins, watering cans and other products.

In the foreseeable future it is likely that quality-assured plastics recyclates will become available, thus making it much easier for designers to use what should be a comparatively cheap material. This trend is being reinforced by governments, many of which are intent on minimising waste. For example, the UK Department of Trade and Industry launched an £11 million research project in 1995 aimed at helping industry develop materials that are easy to recycle.

As recycling gathers pace the availability of inexpensive recyclates is likely to increase. In some cases there is already an oversupply. In the UK, for instance, the quantity of recycled green glass tends to exceed demand, as the UK imports large quantities of green bottles but manufactures comparatively few. This presents an opportunity for designers: even if they cannot persuade consumers to accept milk in green bottles, research by British Glass has suggested that recycled glass could be used for products as varied as garden furniture, bar-room tables, tiles and bricks.

One obvious concern is to avoid the use of toxic substances where this is possible. This, of course, applies to the manufacturing process as well as to the product itself; however, it is far easier to ensure the safe recovery of toxic chemicals within a factory than at the end of the product life. The challenge to the product design team is underlined by research carried out in the State of New Jersey in 1990, which estimated that between 55 per cent and 99 per cent of toxic heavy metals used in manufacturing ended up in products. Some were then substantially recovered and recycled, but by no means all: more than 50 per cent of lead was recovered but nearly all cadmium was released to the environment.

One area for concern is the use of heavy metals in dyes and paints. For example, chromium is often used to bind dye to wool. Change may be forced on the industry through a proposed EU Directive that would limit chromium discharges to 15 milligrams per litre, ten times less than is present in effluents from traditional dyeing methods. There are alternatives: researchers at North Carolina State University have found a way of replacing the heavy metal with iron without damaging either colour- or light-fastness. In general, designers should try to avoid specifying pigments that use heavy metals, such as the use of lead chromates and cadmium-sulphide to produce yellow.

Non-toxic alternatives are being developed for other purposes as well. Blueminster Ltd manufactures a range of non-toxic water-based adhesives that are particularly suitable for the packaging industry. These have cost advantages too, as solvent-based adhesives require three to five times the drying energy and need solvent-recovery systems.

Weight reduction

If any single factor can be isolated as being the most important in meeting environmental objectives it is the reduction of energy consumption. Some materials – virgin aluminium and cement, for instance – are highly energy intensive and their choice can sometimes be the key factor in the overall environmental impact of the product. But this does depend on the nature of the product: a full lifecycle analysis of a vehicle may show that using an energy intensive material such as aluminium can so reduce the weight of the vehicle that savings in the energy used during the vehicle's life far outweigh the additional energy used in manufacturing the material.

One example was the use of aluminium in place of steel in the Audi V8 saloon This reduced the weight of the basic structure of the car by 40 per cent. Of course, this was not achieved without a total design rethink. 'If you have a bumper support assembly in steel weighing 30 pounds and you decide on a piece-for-piece retrofit in aluminium, you can probably get that assembly down to, perhaps, 20 pounds', explained Yale Brandt, Vice-Chairman of Reynolds Metals Company, in an interview in *DESIGN* magazine in 1993. 'If you design a new piece in aluminium using the latest aluminium production technologies and the most appropriate alloy, you can get it down to 15 pounds with no sacrifice in strength or utility – and probably substantial savings in production and assembly costs.'

Weight reduction is a key objective. Using less material obviously saves direct costs as well as minimising the environmental burden. It also has significant knock-on benefits. For example, an over-designed thick wall section moulding requires more material and a longer manufacturing cycle due to longer cooling times of the part. Reducing materials usage should go beyond simply minimising a particular design: alternatives should be considered too. In the case of a thick wall section moulding, it may be possible to achieve the same stiffness by using a ribbed structure instead, thus cutting the quantity of material needed.

Another example of how minimisation can reduce environmental damage (in this case from paint) and save costs is the avoidance of the need for decorative painting by employing a self-coloured material or by using in-mould decoration or textured surfaces.

For some products, weight reduction brings significant benefits during later stages of a product's life. This is especially true of items such as packaging, where lower weight cuts transport costs and can ease handling. But there may be trade-offs. The metal content of some cans has been so reduced by careful design that the proportion of metal to printing ink has been changed to the point where recycling some cans is becoming more difficult.

Checklist

- Ensure that the choice of materials is appropriate to the expected life of the product.
- Use renewable materials from a sustainable source where this is appropriate.
- Use recycled materials if possible.
- Avoid or minimise materials containing toxic chemicals.
- Minimise materials use both by the choice of design approach and through detailed design.
- Consider the energy implications of materials choice over the lifetime of the product.

Manufacturing

Many of the factors that affect the choice of materials also apply to optimising the manufacturing process. Avoiding waste, minimising the use of toxic chemicals, ensuring the efficient use of energy and so on, all apply to designing a product so that it can be manufactured in a way that minimises environmental impact. And, as has been pointed out before, these considerations are generally compatible with overall business efficiency. There is considerable evidence that much more can be done to use resources more efficiently during the manufacturing process. One American study found that, on average, almost twice the quantity (by weight) of materials is thrown away during manufacturing as ends up in the product. Energy consumption figures can be high too: another American study found that it took 2,315 kWh of electricity to manufacture a computer workstation.

Of course, designers often do not have a completely free choice of production processes, being constrained by what is available in the factory that is to make the product. So achieving a design that minimises waste and environmental impact requires the designers to work closely with the production staff and with component suppliers. This is, of course, simple good design practice; but in the environmental context it may mean that the designers have to ensure that factors not previously taken into account in the manufacturing process are considered. There are a number of areas where the design input directly affects efficiency and environmental impact. Four apply quite generally: minimising the variety of materials; avoiding the waste of materials; reducing the number of components and assemblies by integrating functions; and simplifying assembly.

Minimising the materials variety

Minimising the variety of materials used in a product has advantages both in terms of overall business efficiency and the environment. It obviously simplifies ordering and stock-keeping, often with some saving in waste materials. It also simplifies recycling, as there are fewer materials to separate and sort. Indeed, from a recycling point of view a monomaterial product is ideal. For most products this is, of course, impossible. But even where it is possible, design thoughtlessness can remove the advantage. For example, PET is probably the only plastic that can be recycled back to its virgin quality. Many manufacturers of plastics bottles use PET as the only material, making recycling of them easy and worthwhile. But some include a different plastic as a sealing ring: this unnecessary mixing of materials considerably inhibits the recovery of virgin quality PET.

Avoiding waste

Materials can be wasted in all kinds of ways. Where a shape has to be cut from a roll or sheet – whether a vehicle body part, a garment or a label – it is normal practice to ensure that cutting is planned to use the maximum area of the sheet or roll in the finished product; this is made easier if different components use the same sheet or roll specifications as this multiplies the variety of shapes and thus gives greater flexibility in planning to avoid waste. A more subtle cause of waste can be overspecification, as this can lead to an unnecessarily high rate of rejects; designing parts that require excessive care in their handling in order to avoid damage can also increase wastage.

Reducing component numbers

Integrating several functions in one component or assembly can reduce materials use and make savings in tooling and energy. Designing one component to serve more than one purpose – for example, eliminating left and right parts by making them rotationally symmetrical – achieves the same benefits.

Simplifying assembly

Further savings can be made by simplifying the ways in which the finished product is assembled: again, a design that is easy to assemble generally saves money for the manufacturer and is beneficial environmentally, as it is also likely to be simple to disassemble at the end of the product's life (although there are additional design considerations specific to disassembly that will be dealt with later). A design that is easy to assemble and allows good access to components also facilitates servicing and repair, thus helping to extend product life.

Perhaps the most difficult savings to achieve are those where

Figure 4.3 **Flat waste-paper bin**

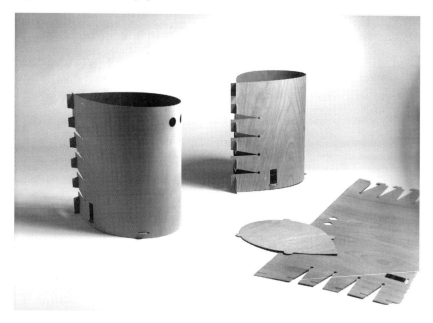

Transport costs are minimised with the Zaket Paperbin, which has been designed in two parts so that it can be delivered flat. Laser-cut from 2 mm beech plywood, the bin can be assembled without tools in just a few seconds. Designer Winfried Scheuer has attempted to ensure that the aesthetics of the design last a long time: 'stylistic obsolescence is an environmental nonsense', she says. The bin is sold through the German Green Party's mail order catalogue. (Winfried Scheuer.)

the problem is not at the forefront of the designers' consideration. So it is always worth trying to find the time to stand back from the project and consider any other efficiency gains that can be made. One area worth considering is the packaging and transport of components or products. While the pack-flat feature of the Zaket Paperbin (see Figure 4.3) is rarely achievable, designing items with nesting geometries can make significant reductions in transport costs and thus reduce pollution too.

Checklist

■ Work with production and component suppliers to choose the

Box 4.1 NCR demonstrates design for environmental and manufacturing efficiency

The NCR 7731 Personal Image Processor prints text and graphics and scans documents, storing their images digitally. The designers have enhanced its intrinsic environmental advantages – reducing the use of paper and eliminating storage and transport – by ensuring that it can be manufactured efficiently, with resulting benefits for profits and the environment.

A common Z-axis assembly plane and extensive use of snap fits eases both manufacture and disassembly by maximising the accessibility of components. Materials variety was minimised by using polyphenylene oxide for all the main cabinetry parts and polycarbonate for internal components. The number of parts was reduced by combining many functions into single integrated moulded components. The modular base allows the addition of optional features, avoiding the production of more features than required by any individual customer.

The designers have also aimed to conserve resources in the design of the packaging both of components and of the finished product. Parts packaging is re-usable and is returned to suppliers by NCR; customers are encouraged to recycle the product packaging by the design of unpacking procedures supported by obvious documentation explaining what to do.

All the effort to maximise efficiency increased the design costs of the processor. But this has paid off. For instance, the extra time needed to design a more complex part has cut the manufacturing time that would have been required to put together many simpler parts. Design time itself was minimised by using solids modelling to maximise the functionality of a part's features accurately; CAD techniques such as finite element analysis and interference checking added to the feasibility of using this design approach.

'Good ecological sense also makes good business sense. Many cost, quality, schedule, manufacturing and serviceability criteria coincided with environmental goals', was NCR's conclusion at the end of the design project.

---

least environmentally damaging manufacturing processes available.

■ Minimise the variety of materials used.

■ Design to avoid materials wastage.

■ Reduce the number of components and assemblies by integrating functions.

■ Design for simple assembly.

5 The design considerations: use and end-of-life

■ Introduction ■ End-of-life

Introduction

The phase of product life that often gets too little attention when considering the environmental impacts of a product is use – designers have instead tended to concentrate on the manufacturing and disposal stages. For some products, these more traditional priorities are correct – the use of everything from furniture and tableware to garden tools and bicycles has minimal environmental impact compared with the manufacturing and end-of-life phases of their lives (durability and life extension are dealt with here as end-of-life matters). But for other products – domestic appliances, office machinery, vehicles and so on – it can be the use stage that causes the most environmental damage and that deserves the greatest attention from the design team.

But before looking at these high-impact-in-use products it is worth pointing out that there is a third category of products that have little direct environmental impact in use but that can cause indirect problems. The best example is clothing. Clothes are innocuous in environmental terms in use, but washing or dry cleaning them is usually damaging to the environment. There are two issues for the design team. First, does the design allow comparatively benign methods of cleaning, without the use of solvents or high temperature washing, for example. Second, does the design discourage excessive cleaning: Dorothy Mackenzie, in her book *Green Design – Design for the Environment*,[1] pointed the finger at the leading fashion designer Rifat Ozbek, who jumped on the Green bandwagon with a self-styled 'eco-fashion' range that featured an array of pure white clothes that were not only bleached but also required continual cleaning.

These factors recede into insignificance when considering the environmental impacts made by the use of other kinds of product, especially those that consume significant amounts of energy. In the domestic sector, heating appliances, cars, refrigerators and freezers, light fittings, air-conditioning equipment, cookers and washing machines (see Table 5.1) all cause the great majority of their lifetime environmental impacts when in use. Where such products consume not just energy but other materials too, then the importance of the use stage can be even greater.

Washing machines, for example, consume energy, water and detergent. A lifecycle analysis of washing machines – carried out by PA Consulting as part of the preparatory work for the European Community's Ecolabel scheme – split the life of a washing machine into four stages: production, distribution, use and disposal, and examined the environmental impact made at each stage on energy consumption, air pollution, water pollution, solid waste and water consumption. The results showed that the overwhelming proportion of the impacts came from the use stage of the machine's life, not from manufacture or disposal. Well over 90 per cent of the solid wastes and air and water pollution produced during the life of a washing machine came from its use, with energy and water consumption being similarly concentrated

Table 5.1 Cradle-to-grave assessment of environmental impacts of washing machines

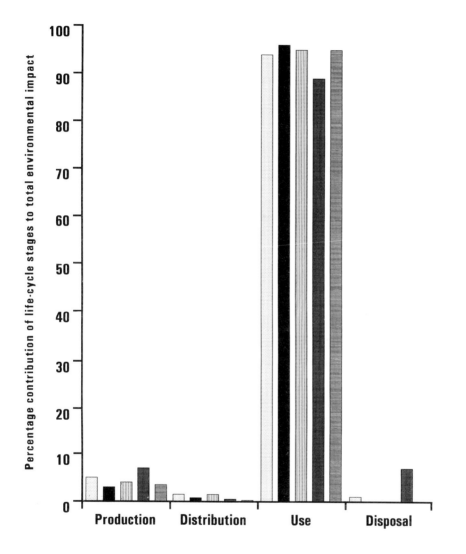

A lifecycle assessment of the environmental impacts of washing machines shows that the vast majority of the impacts occur during the use stage of machine life.

in this phase of the machine's life. In environmental terms, the materials and processes used to make a washing machine, how it is packaged and transported, and whether it is recycled or not are almost irrelevant compared with how it performs in use.

Crucial role of design

The PA study had a second important message, for it demonstrated clearly the crucial role that designers can play in reducing environmental impacts. For the differences in environmental performance between the best and worst machines studied was considerable, with the best using half the water and energy of the worst; and when it came to detergent loss, the differences were even more notable, with the worst losing 30 times more than the best.

While a major contribution to the improved performance of washing machines is due to innovation, attention to detailed design improvements is vital too. One of the best performing refrigerators is made by the Danish manufacturer Gram and is the result of careful design rather than any technological breakthrough: it uses good insulation, effective and long-lasting door seals, and efficient motors and heat exchangers.

Of course, the benefits from greater efficiency are felt not just in the environment but by the consumer too. As Table 5.2 shows, the extra costs of such products can payback in energy savings within a year or two (Table 5.2 applies to average products: the lifetime payback for going from the worst performing product to the best performing can more than cover the cost of the new machine).

Not all new products are more energy-efficient than those they replace. Car manufacturers have spent a great deal of effort improving the fuel efficiency of their vehicles, achieving an

Table 5.2 **Payback for energy-efficient appliances**

	Extra cost (£s)	Average energy use (kWh a year)	Decrease in energy use (%)	Time to recoup cost (in years)
Dishwasher	20	500	40	1.4
Fridge	35	300	80	2.1
Freezer	42	740	65	1.2
Kettle	0	250	20	0

Source: UK Energy Efficiency Office (1990)

average improvement of around 40 per cent over the last ten years for a same-specification model. Despite this, Sweden's vehicle testing authority has suggested that the improved energy efficiency of new cars is more than offset by the energy used to manufacture them compared with maintaining longer-life cars; this view is confirmed by experience in the UK, where the average car sold today actually consumes more fuel than a decade ago as buyers look for bigger cars and extra energy-consuming equipment such as electric windows, more lights and air-conditioning. Similar effects can be seen in other product areas: frost-free refrigerators use more energy than conventional models; the average new vacuum cleaner uses more energy than the one it replaces; and power showers – unlike ordinary showers – can use even more water than a bath.

Far from being a reason for designers to ignore the need to minimise energy and other resource use, this trend makes efficiency-in-use even more important. Energy costs are bound to increase in the future as governments take action to tackle the threat of global warming and climate change (several governments have already taken action to raise petrol prices for this reason) and energy efficiency is therefore likely to become an increasingly important factor when consumers choose which product to buy. This trend will be spurred by the spread of energy labelling.

Guiding the customer

There is another important implication for designers: how the product is used by the consumer can be a key factor in the environmental performance of a product. For example, there is not much point in scientists developing low-temperature detergents and designers devising washing machine programmes that utilise these to cut energy costs if the user does not understand the advantages and continues to wash at traditional temperatures. Instruction books are important but not always read, which is why the EU Ecolabel criteria for washing machines includes a requirement for advice on wash selection to be a permanent feature of the machine's controls. Going one stage further, designers should consider making the most efficient programme the default setting on this kind of equipment.

The importance of energy efficiency is, if anything, even greater for products used in commerce and industry. For example, research by the UK's Building Research Establishment has shown that personal computers can add more to the office electricity bill than heating or lighting. For powered office equipment generally, there can be a double benefit for a company in purchasing energy-efficient equipment: it not only cuts electricity bills and pollution directly but, because it gives out less heat, it also minimises the costs of air-conditioning. Similar considerations apply to capital goods, where purchasers often need no persuasion to look for reduced running costs when purchasing equipment.

Using waste energy

There is, though, one important difference between designing for the ordinary consumer and designing for a commercial user. In general, the direct recovery and re-use of waste energy or other resources lost in use is unlikely to be economic for most domestic products (although it is becoming a feature of items such as domestic air extractors). But the capture and re-use of resources can be of considerable interest to a commercial user, both in meeting environmental requirements and in saving money. Such systems range from incorporating regenerative braking into electric vehicles so that energy is returned to the batteries to utilising a centrifuge to decontaminate cutting fluids so that they can be re-used.

Checklist

- Minimise the use of energy and other resources required by a product to perform its function.
- Design both the product and accompanying instruction manuals to encourage its most efficient use.
- Consider how waste energy and other resources can be recycled and utilised.

End-of-life costs can be considerable: see Table 5.3. Although manufacturers do not currently have to meet these costs, this situation is changing, with legislation already signalled that will place responsibility for safe disposal onto the manufacturer for certain products. So anything that designers can do to minimise disposal costs is likely to pay off in the future.

End-of-life

When considering the final stages of a product's life, the first question designers should ask is 'What is the ideal life for this

Table 5.3 The cost of disposal

Disposal costs as a share of total product lifetime costs

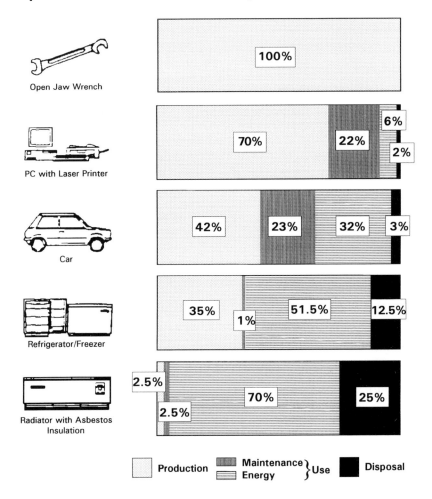

Source: Fraunhofer-Institut für Produktionstechnik und Automatisierung

particular product in terms of minimising overall environmental impact?' 'As long as possible' may seem the obvious response. Although this may be true for most products, this answer does need some qualifications.

First, for products that make their major impacts during the use stage of their life, technological and design improvements can mean that there is an environmental advantage in replacing an older, less-efficient product even before it has reached the end of its life (as with some of the domestic appliances mentioned in the previous section). This does not mean that such products should be designed with deliberately short lives but that it may not be worth using extra materials or manufacturing resources to increase product life.

This leads directly to the second consideration. Increasing product life may mean using thicker sections or additional components to resist wear and tear. In these cases, the further environmental burdens at the manufacturing stage need to be balanced against the savings made by postponing the purchase of a replacement product. This equation is complicated when the extra weight leads to other environmental impacts; a heavier car will, for example, be less fuel efficient. How the design team can resolve these and similar questions will be looked at in the next chapter.

Finally, there are some products that have a specific lifespan as part of their function – medicine capsules would not work if they did not dissolve; and newspapers have a finite life too. In such cases, the short life expectancy can be exploited by, for example, using relatively poor quality paper for newsprint.

In recent years, much of the emphasis on end-of-life issues has been on recycling. Recycling has its place, but it is some way down the hierarchy. The hierarchy I have adopted in this section is: durability, upgradability, re-use, recycling and, finally, disposal.

Durability

Independent studies suggest that product life has been getting shorter, despite manufacturers' claims: today's cookers, vacuum cleaners, kettles and irons are less durable than their predecessors[2] (estimates of current product life spans are shown in Table 5.4). There are also indications that consumers are more ready to throw products away for reason of fashion or minor damage that might, in less wealthy times, have been retained. One study of domestic appliances thrown away at municipal waste disposal sites showed that a quarter were still functioning and another quarter needed just minor repairs.

On the other hand, there are examples of companies that have deliberately set out to design more durable products and have benefited as a result. For instance, ASKO, the Finnish white goods manufacturer, claims that its washing machines are designed to last for 15 years and offers a five year parts and labour guarantee. Linn, the successful Scottish hi-fi manufacturer, designs its products for long-term upgradability. Land Rovers last, on average, 30 years, while Volvo and Saab increased the average lifespan of their cars from 9 years to 16 years between 1965 and

Table 5.4 **Product lifespans**

Product	Lifespan (years)
Cars	11–12
Cookers	10–15
Washing machines	7–10
Refrigerators	10–12
Microwaves	8–10
Radio cassette players	10
Telephones	3
Televisions	10

Source: New Economics Foundation (1994) *Beyond Recycling*

Box 5.1 Kyocera provides long-life benefits

The Japanese computer printer manufacturer Kyocera broke into the European market by promising lower costs and improved environmental performance with its 'Ecosys' range featuring long-life drums and cartridges. Kyocera claims that its ceramic drums last twice as long as conventional drums, halving the running costs of its printer compared with its main rival.

1982, winning them 40 per cent of the Swedish market partly because of the ability of their cars to resist harsh climatic conditions. At the same time, some other car manufacturers lost market share after well-reported durability failures, particularly body rusting.

There are no official product durability standards in place except as part of safety regulations and the EU Ecolabel scheme does not include durability as a criteria. Dorothy Mackenzie, Director of the Dragon International design consultancy and leading authority on Green design, believes that this is no reason for inaction. 'Designers should think beyond the legislation to what makes environmental sense', she says. Her view is supported by the likelihood that some regulations on product durability will be introduced: the Netherlands government is just one that is considering such a move.

The durability of a product depends on a number of design factors. The starting point is, of course, the identification and elimination of potential weak points in the design. For operational parts – whether mechanical, electrical or electronic – conventional statistical reliability targets can be set in 'mean time between failure' terms.

For passive components, the design team needs to be aware of the potential causes of damage and take reasonable precautions to minimise the need for repair. This means looking at how the product is going to be treated in reality, which is sometimes very different from the way the product is intended to be used. For example, a playground swing may be intended for a toddler to sit safely in an enclosed seat; in practice, it may have to cope with a heavy teenager climbing the frame or even attempting to vandalise the equipment and the design team needs to ensure that the swing is designed to resist these kinds of common abuse. Where to draw the line between designing for common misuse and ensuring that the product will endure the most extreme use is a decision that depends on a mix of factors, ranging from safety to expense.

Ease of maintenance and repair are also important factors in ensuring that a product achieves its expected design life. Many of the design features that facilitate this also assist such objectives as simplicity of assembly during manufacture and disassembly for recycling. Good access to components that may need replacement and ensuring that they can be removed easily are essential. Components that may need replacement should, as far as possible, not be integrated with others in a way that requires more to be replaced than is really necessary.

Users should be encouraged to repair products. Instruction books should not only include clear fault identification rituals but should, where appropriate, encourage knowledgeable users to undertake simple repairs themselves, providing safety is not put at risk. The inclusion of microprocessors in an ever-widening range of products is enlarging the opportunities for including self-diagnostic programs. Where feasible these should be designed to help the user as well as the professional repairer. Even if they merely enable the user to give details of the fault to the repairer when calling him or her out, this can assist in estimating the likely cost – and thus prevent the user being discouraged from considering repair by the open-cheque worries created by some repair horror stories – and ensure that the correct parts are brought. One manufacturer that has utilised such a system is the domestic boiler manufacturer Vaillant Ltd: its 'Ecomax' boiler incorporates an electronic system and an LCD display to provide comprehensive information to assist installation, commissioning and servicing. For example, the fault mode displays codes indicating such problems as no gas supply.

The scope for increasing product life by encouraging repair is demonstrated by the study referred to earlier of domestic appliances retrieved from rubbish tips: some had been thrown away simply because the fuse had blown. However, the path to improved repairability is not entirely straightforward, as it runs counter to some other legislative pressures. For example, the development of throw-away, non-repairable products has been encouraged in the United States by legal liability concerns about the potential for accidents to people carrying out repairs.

Possibly even more fraught as far as designers are concerned is the question of fashion redundancy. This can apply as much to kitchen furniture and bicycles as to clothes and soft furnishings. Indeed, the Austrian psychologist Leonard Oberascher has suggested that

> A general tendency of today is that the functional value or usefulness of a product becomes gradually less important to the consumer. He seldom buys a product only because of its functionality or price but because of its symbolic value. By purchasing a product he acquires a piece of image, hoping that the product's aura will also throw some light on his personality. Hence industrial products more and more fulfil the role of cultural symbols.[3]

While designers, even if they wanted to, do not have the power
to persuade the public to accept the kind of anti-consumerist idyll
so beloved of some Deep Green environmentalists, they can play
a part in countering the trend towards replacing products ever
more frequently for 'keeping up with the Joneses' reasons. They
can, for example, avoid attaching short-lived fashion icon features
to products that should be long-lived; this may mean avoiding
extreme-but-trendy colours on kitchen cabinets or simply
designing some items in a more neutral way. A different and, for
some products, more effective way of ensuring product durability
is simply to make the item so attractive that no one wants to throw
it away: the antiques world shows how good design can be long
valued and long lasting.

Upgradability

Durability is not the only factor in extending the life of a product.
Designing to facilitate upgrading is becoming an important
selling point for equipment where the technology is improving at
a rapid rate, such as with computers. With products like these, the
rate of technological development and the increasing demands of
users does not require the replacement of every component:
power supplies, motherboards, cases, keyboards and so on do not
have to be changed to give extra speed or storage capacity. So
designing the machines so that memory chips can be added,
increased disk storage installed and the main processor chip
upgraded makes considerable sense for the purchaser, as well as
saving resources and helping the environment.

Much the same approach can be taken to products such as
audio equipment, where innovation tends to come with the
introduction of new tape and CD formats or the extension of
digital broadcasting; the speed of development in these areas is

far faster than improvements in loudspeakers and amplifiers, making upgradability a major benefit for the user.

Upgradability may well have a part to play in many products that use microprocessors, from central heating systems to washing machines. The advantages of more sophisticated heating controls in cutting fuel bills and improving comfort are becoming more widely recognised: a controller designed so that additional modules can be added as either cash or need demands would have obvious appeal. If such a controller could be expanded to provide other services – automatic control of lighting or security systems, for instance – then the product's potential may be vastly increased.

A potential problem of designing products such as washing machines to have a longer life is that the rate of development of detergents and changes in fabric types may make them obsolete while they are still in good working order. For instance, environmental and cost pressures to reduce energy use may well lead to the introduction of detergents that will wash satisfactorily with a long cold water cycle. Such detergents could not be used in most existing machines. But almost all modern washing machine programmers are microprocessor-based, which should provide the facility for comparatively easy upgrading to cope with whatever demands for new wash-cycle programs arise in the future. An example of a domestic product – a refrigerator – that has been designed to facilitate upgrading is shown in Figure 5.1.

Psychologist Leonard Oberascher points out that non-technical products can be upgraded too. 'Colour is a powerful tool to alter the symbolic value of a product,' he says and goes on to point out that, while trend colours can be used as a means to accelerate product lifecycles, they can also be used to extend product life if used as an upgrade. Re-upholstering furniture in a

Figure 5.1 **Advantages of modular design**

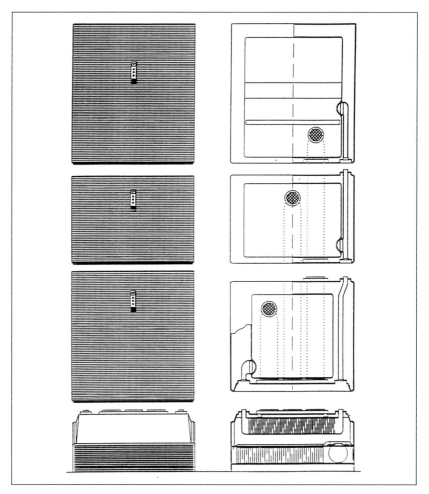

'Green Frost' is the name given to a demonstration project to show the advantages of modular design. The work of the Italian plastics manufacturer ECP EniChem Polimeri and the Domus Academy, the concept refrigerator uses a common base unit housing the compressor on to which can be fitted a variety of storage units. Not only does this approach simplify manufacture and recycling but it also facilitates repair and upgrading with alternative storage modules. All the cabinet components – the external cabinet, the foam insulation (which is CFC-free), the inner liner and the accessories – are made from materials belonging to the same polymer family, styrenics. The recycled material can be re-used in the primary production process and this approach to materials also simplifies manufacture by integrating the production of the styrenic components into a single cycle, radically reducing assembly operations. (Domus Academy.)

new fabric is a traditional way in which such upgrading has been carried out, but upgrading to a modern colour could equally well apply, for example, to kitchen cabinets if the panels were designed to be changed easily.

From the manufacturer's point of view, designing for upgrading can lead to a real commercial advantage, for it can lock the purchaser into buying upgrades from the original manufacturer rather than buying an entirely new model (or kitchen) from a rival.

Design for upgrading seems likely to be of growing importance in the future.

Re-use

Even when products come to the end of their life, they may be capable of being used for another purpose, as any visit to a third world country will rapidly show. While second uses are not entirely unknown in the West – there have, for example, been jams packed in jars that can later be used as drinking glasses – it is more usual for parts or components to be re-used.

In some industries, refurbishment and re-use has become an accepted procedure. Many lorry diesel engines, for example, are refurbished and re-used and systems for collecting and re-using computer printer cartridges are well established, being facilitated in the UK by the formation of a Cartridge Recyclers' Association that has set minimum standards, helping the market top one million units in 1994.

Recovered components are sometimes unsuitable for re-use for their original purpose, especially in technologically fast-moving industries. This need not rule out re-use, as other industries may not require the performance of the very latest technology: thus microprocessors and memory chips recovered from old computers can be perfectly adequate for electronic toys: ICL is just one company selling on recovered chips for this purpose.

Re-use and refurbishment is especially attractive to companies that lease products rather than sell them outright. Photocopiers are often refurbished at the end of a lease, upgraded if necessary, and then re-leased.

From the point of view of the design team, the concerns relating to re-use are no different from the concerns of other stages of the product lifecycle, the most crucial being ease of disassembly either to assist the refurbishment of the complete product or to allow components to be removed without damage for re-use.

Recycling

While re-use is concerned with recovering complete products or components, recycling seeks to recover useful raw materials. There are three basic design objectives in facilitating recycling: to ensure that different materials can easily be separated; to enable the easy identification of different materials; and to avoid as far as possible difficulties from the cross-contamination of incompatible materials.

Except with monomaterial products – which are, of course, the great joy of recyclers – recycling starts with breaking up the product as far as possible into its separate materials. So the first decision for the design team is whether disassembly should be by reverse assembly or brute force. If there is any likelihood of recycling being combined with the re-use of any components, then reverse assembly is the only choice. In this case, the design team should ensure that fastening points are clearly marked and accessible. If brute force is the chosen approach, the main requirement is the ability to grasp the parts to be separated

---

Box 5.2 Conflicting aspirations

Different environmental objectives can be in conflict with each other. For example, the tightening of regulations to protect computer users from electromagnetic radiation has led some manufacturers to meet the requirements by spraying a metal coating on to the plastics case to provide a radiation shield. Unfortunately, this prevents the case from being recycled. One way round this is for the designer to use a separate metal shield. But the best answer is to tackle the problem at source, by designing the printed circuit board to minimise radiation so that no shield is necessary.

---

combined with fastenings that are designed to break apart at defined positions. Some ways of designing for disassembly are illustrated in Figure 5.2.

As explained earlier, the inability to easily separate incompatible materials is the bane of a recycler's life, especially when plastics are mixed. But the problem is not confined to plastics: copper is extremely difficult to remove in the steel recycling process, and a mere 0.2 per cent of copper can cause severe cracking in the finished steel. So designing wiring harnesses so that they can be easily separated and removed from, for example, domestic appliances significantly simplifies recycling.

Care should also be taken to ensure that plastics parts are not designed in a way that prevents their easy separation from other materials. Moulded-in metal reinforcements and rivets can cause problems; if screws are used, they should ideally be made from the same material as the component they are holding. Some plastics are compatible in recycling, although the resultant raw material will not, of course, have the same qualities as virgin material. Table 5.5 (page 110) indicates compatibility. Even where materials can be separated relatively easily, it helps the recycler if compatible materials are used. For instance, if the same

Figure 5.2 **Designing for disassembly**

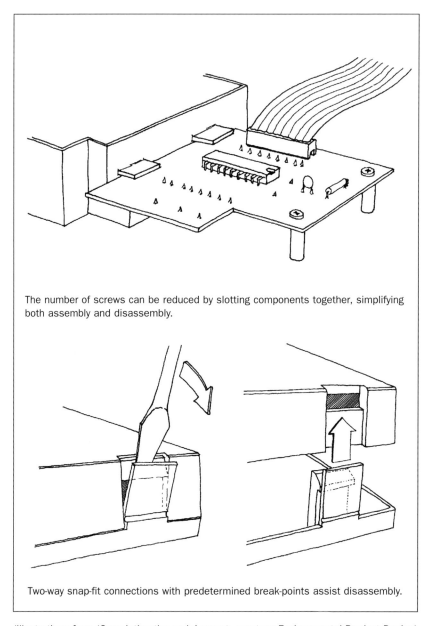

The number of screws can be reduced by slotting components together, simplifying both assembly and disassembly.

Two-way snap-fit connections with predetermined break-points assist disassembly.

(Illustrations from 'Completing the cycle' report, courtesy Environmental Product Design)

Box 5.3 **Fully recyclable bath**

ICI Acrylics and Showerlux have combined to develop the first fully-recyclable acrylic bath. The system is based on an ICI-patented process that enables acrylic baths and shower trays to be separated into their two principal components, the acrylic sheet and the GRP/FRP reinforcement. The recovered acrylic material is recycled by ICI, while the reinforcement material is re-used by Showerlux in its bath manufacturing process, thus completing the recycling loop.

---

material is used for the skin and the insulation in a refrigerator, the recycler can cut out one separation operation.

Adhesives can cause recycling problems, especially with plastics. Alternatives such as ultrasonic welding, heat staking, spin welding or hot-plate or hot-gas welding should be considered instead. Paints and labels can also cause problems with plastics: better alternatives are laser-printed texts and icons; hot stamping; or labels using the same plastics material.

Automatic systems for sorting plastics are being developed. One, using infra-red radiation, has been developed at the Sandia National Laboratories in New Mexico: it can sort with almost 100 per cent accuracy all the main recyclable plastics, including PET, two types of polyethylene, polyvinyl chloride, polystyrene and polypropylene. Nevertheless, such equipment is unlikely to be widely used in the near future and designers should still ensure that plastics materials are permanently marked with either an identifying bar code or by moulding-in the recognised material symbol. The aim of all recycling is to degrade the material as little as possible. Although some degradation is inevitable with almost all plastics recycling, minimising degradation by the careful separation of plastics into those that are compatible minimises such debasement. Careful design allied with reliable recycling practices can enable plastics to be used a number of times, with

Table 5.5 Compatibility of polymers for recycling

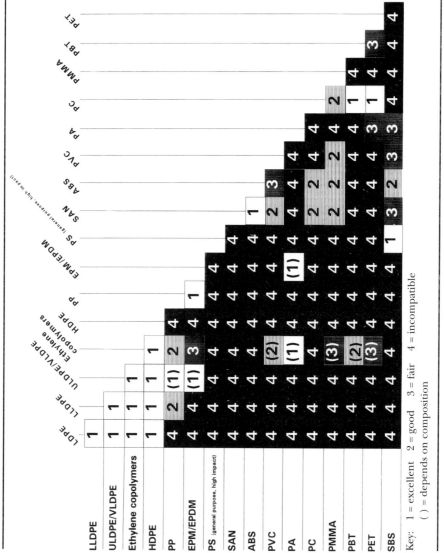

	LDPE	LLDPE	ULDPE/VLDPE	Ethylene copolymers	HDPE	PP	EPM/EPDM	PS (general purpose, high impact)	SAN	ABS	PVC	PA	PC	PMMA	PBT	PET
LLDPE	1															
ULDPE/VLDPE	1	1														
Ethylene copolymers	1	1	1													
HDPE	1	1	1	1												
PP	4	2	2 (1)	2	4											
EPM/EPDM	4	4	4 (1)	3	4	4										
PS (general purpose, high impact)	4	4	4	4	4	4	4									
SAN	4	4	4	4	4	4	4	4								
ABS	4	4	4	4	4	4	4	4	1							
PVC	4	4	4 (2)	4 (2)	4	4	4	4	2	3						
PA	4	4	4 (1)	4 (1)	4	4 (1)	4	4	2	4	4					
PC	4	4	4	4	4	4	4	4	2	2	4	4				
PMMA	4	4	4 (3)	4 (3)	4	4	4	4	2	2	2	4	2			
PBT	4	4	4 (2)	4 (2)	4	4	4	4	2	2	2	4	1	4		
PET	4	4	4 (3)	4 (3)	4	4	4	4	4	4	4	3	1	4	3	
SBS	4	4	4	4	4	4	4	1	3	2	3	3	4	4	4	4

Key: 1 = excellent   2 = good   3 = fair   4 = incompatible   ( ) = depends on composition

Source: Dow Plastics

the quality cascading down only a little on each occasion.

If designers are in a position to be able to use the different qualities of plastics as they cascade through a closed system, this is the ideal way of minimising materials loss. This can be done by creating a downgradable application; a car design team may, for example, be able to design the floor of the luggage compartment or the cover for the inside of a wheel arch to use the plastic recovered from, say, a car bumper.

The most effective design for recycling comes from close co-operation between the design team and the recycler. This, of course, is not possible for many products, where the design team – for the moment at least – has little idea where the product will end up when its life is finished. However, some companies have been able to develop such relationships: IBM UK has a contractual relationship with the Mann Organisation in which the price paid by Mann for the end-of-life products depends on the profitability of its recycling operation. This creates an incentive to change product design to facilitate recycling and helps the designers by providing feedback about recycling problems.

In the future, the links between design and recycling may be made somewhat easier for many manufacturers with the setting up of industry responsibility groups aimed at establishing recycling systems for specific industries. Some nine such groups are being established in the UK and similar approaches are being taken in a number of other European countries too.

Disposal

It is not, of course, possible to re-use or recycle every product or component. Inevitably, some will end up being disposed of either in a landfill dump or, increasingly, in an incinerator from which some energy can be recovered and used (the potential for energy

Table 5.6 **Calorific value of various materials**

Material	Calorific value (KJ/kg)
Mixed plastics	37,000
Polystyrene	46,000
Polyethylene	46,000
PVC	18,900
Heating oil	44,000
Coal	30,000
Wood	16,000

Source: Dow Plastics

recovery is demonstrated in Table 5.6). The main design consideration at this final stage in the life of a product is to ensure that, whatever disposal method is utilised, the materials in the product do not create a hazard.

Ideally, this means avoiding heavy metals and toxic substances, although – as usual with design – a balance sometimes has to be struck between allowing some contamination in exchange for more substantial environmental gains. For example, energy efficient compact fluorescent light bulbs are so much better in terms of reducing greenhouse gas emissions from power stations that the fact that they contain mercury tends to be overlooked.

A manufacturer's responsibility can go somewhat further. For example, vehicle airbags are powered by between 50 and 150 grams of sodium azide which converts into harmless nitrogen gas on impact. But if scrapped unused, this chemical can easily convert into highly toxic hydrazoic acid. So the manufacturer should ensure that the airbags are deployed before the vehicle is shredded, in this case probably by ensuring that vehicle scrap operators are informed of the danger and trained to deal with it. For potentially hazardous products that should ideally not be landfilled – batteries or paint tins, for example – the manufacturer should take all reasonable steps to encourage consumers to adopt environmentally-sound disposal methods (for example, battery recycling schemes do exist, and some refuse collection authorities are increasingly providing methods for separately collecting hazardous wastes); this means giving advice prominently on the product and in any instruction leaflet.

Designers do, of course, have available to them a range of so-called biodegradable materials. Some of these do not, in practice, degrade fully, relying, for example, on a web of non-biodegradable plastics to give strength to the degradable material. Others – such as ICI's Biopol, which is made by a bacterium from the fermentation of sugars – are truly biodegradable, breaking down into carbon dioxide and water. But even these totally biodegradable materials have substantial disadvantages: if mixed in with the normal waste stream, they can inhibit recycling; and they degrade very slowly, doing little for the litter problem that is a prime cause of complaints about packaging. So designers are best advised to restrict such materials to uses where the degradability provides an advantage that cannot be provided in any other way.

Checklist

- Examine what is the ideal life for a particular product and as far as possible design to achieve this.
- Review product designs to identify and eliminate potential weaknesses.
- Ensure that the product is easy to maintain and repair.
- Ensure that instruction manuals and information on the product encourage repair.
- Avoid over-trendy designs that encourage too-early product replacement.
- Design to facilitate upgrading.

- Consider how the product is to be disassembled.
- Check that any fixing methods and finishes do not inhibit recycling.
- Ensure that plastics components carry permanent identification of materials.
- Investigate whether a chain can be set up to ensure a cascade system for utilising recycled plastics.
- Ensure that materials do not create a hazard on disposal.

6 Environmental design tools

Introduction

The last two chapters identified the many points in the life of a product where design can influence environmental impact. This chapter looks at some of the tools available to designers to help them minimise the environmental impacts of the products they develop. Of course, traditional design skills and techniques are far from redundant in environmentally-conscious design. But environmentally-conscious design does make new demands on the design team. The most important – and the one that designers find most difficult – is the identification and measurement of environmental impact. This must, of course, be the basis for all design decisions aimed at reducing the environmental damage. Most of this chapter is therefore devoted to methods of assessing environmental impact.

Does it matter for this product?

Before embarking on an often complex analysis of environmental impacts, the first question the design team should ask is 'Is environmental impact likely to be a serious factor in the design of this product?' It is possible to argue that environmental considerations should never be ignored, however minimal the effects, as the sum of numerous tiny impacts may add up to something that is significant. However, the environmental consequences of manufacturing small batches of specialist pieces of furniture or jewellery, for example, do not justify any real design commitment to impact minimisation, although the designer may choose to give the issue some thought for personal ethical reasons.

At the beginning of any design project it is therefore worth asking where the particular product falls in the hierarchy of environmental importance and, consequently, how much attention needs to be paid to designing to minimise environmental damage. There are four key considerations in making such an assessment. The first is quantity. If the individual product is resource intensive (such as a building) or if it is going to be manufactured in large quantities (such as a crisp packet), then environmental issues are critical. The second consideration is energy. If significant quantities of energy are expended in making the product or if it consumes meaningful amounts of energy in use, the design team cannot ignore these impacts. Third is the question of risk. If the product involves hazardous substances in any way or if its reliability is essential to minimise environmental hazard, the design team must pay detailed attention to these factors. This means that environmental considerations can be critical in the design even of computer software: the energy and materials used in producing, distributing and using the software may be infinitesimal, but if the failure of the software might, for instance, result in an oil-tanker going aground, then its design is clearly environmentally crucial.

The final question concerns environmental sensitivity and is more subjective. It concerns not so much the inherent characteristics of the product or materials as the context in which they are used or acquired. For example, tropical hardwoods can be grown on a sustainable basis with comparatively little environmental damage; however, at the moment their acquisition usually results in the destruction of irreplaceable rainforest and its associated genetic resources and, frequently, consequential land erosion and river silting. If a product development team suspects that its activities may have some bearing on such issues, it should take steps to investigate properly.

Where a design project fits into this hierarchy it can provide a useful, if rough and ready, guide to the way in which environmental issues are tackled.

The role of lifecycle analysis

The prime tool for assessing the environmental impact of a product is lifecycle analysis (LCA). LCA is far from rough and ready: it aims to provide a statistical inventory of the total impacts made during the complete life of the product, from the cradle to the grave, from the acquisition of materials to final disposal. Table 6.1 shows the basic evaluation matrix used for deciding the criteria for the EU Ecolabel scheme.

Lifecycle analysis is never simple and the amount of information gathered can rapidly get out of hand. Table 6.2 shows an evaluation matrix generated during the development of possible Ecolabel criteria for a coffee-maker. Twenty-five types of environmental impact are listed and cross-referenced to five stages of the product's life.

Two points are immediately obvious: first, even for a comparatively simple product such as a small domestic appliance,

Table 6.1 **Basic Ecolabel lifecycle analysis matrix**

	Supply (materials, etc.)	Production	Distribution	Use	Disposal
Air contamination					
Water contamination					
Soil contamination					
Waste					
Energy consumption					
Local habitat					

Source: UK Ecolabelling Board

carrying out a full LCA is complex and time-consuming. Second, this particular evaluation matrix includes entirely different kinds of data, from factual numerate measures such as 'Total quantity of emissions from energy consumed' to the far more subjective 'Depletion of nature/landscape/quality of the physical environment'.

Energy sources

There are other problems too. For example, the energy emissions will vary depending on the source of the energy: hydro-generated electricity, for instance, will produce little in the way of emissions to air but may have a significant effect on landscape quality while electricity from a coal-fired power station will produce significant emissions to air as well as having a landscape component. Similar wide variations in impact can come from different sources of the same material: recycled aluminium has far less damaging impacts than aluminium from virgin sources.

Table 6.2 Evaluation matrix for Ecolabel for coffee-maker (continued overleaf)

			Extraction of raw materials	Material production	Manufacture	Use	Disposal
Resources and raw materials	1	Exhaustion of scarce renewable raw materials					
	2	Exhaustion of non-renewable raw materials					
	3	Total quantity of raw materials used					
Energy	4	Exhaustion of non-renewable sources of energy					
	5	Total quantity of emissions from energy consumed					
Emissions	6	Emissions of acidifying compounds					
	7	Emissions of eutrophying substances					
	8	Emissions of greenhouse gases					
	9	Emissions of ozone-depleting substances					
	10	Emissions of substances toxic to flora and fauna					
	11	Emissions of substances toxic to human beings					
	12	Emissions of waste heat					
	13	Release of radiation					

Table 6.2 (concluded)

			Extraction of raw materials	Material production	Manufacture	Use	Disposal
Nuisance	14	Release of stench and odour					
	15	Noise nuisance for the user/environment					
	16	Danger of disasters					
	17	Depletion of nature/landscape/quality of the physical environment					
Waste	18	Quantity of waste before processing					
	19	Quantity of waste after processing (final waste)					
	20	Quantity of chemical waste					
Recyclability	21	Recyclability of total product					
	22	Recyclability of product parts					
	23	Recyclability of materials					
Repairability	24	Repairability of the product					
Life	25	Technical life of the product					

Source: Netherlands Ministry of Housing

Carrying out the LCA itself is not the only challenge. Evaluating and using the information it produces can be just as difficult. It is all very well to know that one design produces higher lifetime sulphur dioxide emissions but lower carbon monoxide emissions than an alternative, but how do you evaluate which choice is less damaging? LCA is no panacea. But it is a useful tool if properly directed.

Different kinds of LCA

There are, in fact, several quite different uses of LCA. One is in setting standards within a regulatory or formal assessment procedure, such as ecolabelling. Here, the process needs to be thorough in order both to identify the critical criteria for a particular product category and to decide the level at which to set the maximum allowable impacts. While the results of this use of LCA are of considerable interest to product developers, the process itself is primarily the concern of the regulatory bodies.

For the product design team, LCA has three main uses. The first is in distinguishing the key environmental impacts of a particular product. This does not generally require a high degree of refinement. The aim is to identify both the environmentally most important stages in the product lifecycle and the main environmental impacts which the designers need to concentrate on during the design process. This is crucial, for the most important issues are not always obvious. As was shown in Chapter 5, a thorough LCA carried out during the development of the ecolabel criteria for washing machines showed that designers could, from the environmental impact point of view, virtually ignore the materials, manufacture and disposal stages of the product lifecycle, for almost all the damage is caused during the use stage of the machine (see Table 5.1 on page 91).

Deciding which approach

The use of an LCA to make broad assessments can also be valuable in helping to decide between alternative approaches to a particular problem. For example, the LCA of a coffee-maker carried out within the matrix shown in Table 6.2 gave designers of such appliances two useful directions: it showed that the key environmental design areas for attention were energy consumption in use and the impacts of paper filters; and it indicated that non-electrical coffee-makers scored consistently badly on energy consumption.

The other main use of LCA for the product developer is in refining a design. For this purpose, the LCA needs to be reasonably accurate but its focus can be narrowed down to the key areas identified earlier. An example of this use is given in Table 6.3, which shows comparative assessments for a car bumper using a variety of materials. Here, energy consumption has been chosen as the key environmental factor. The fuel used by a car is by far the single largest cause of environmental damage during the cradle-to-grave life of the vehicle; this is reflected in this particular LCA by the inclusion of a 'use' component in the

Table 6.3 **LCA of car bumper designs**

Material	SMC	ALU	Fe	PPO/PA	PUR	Mod.PET	Units
Weight	4.96	3.84	7.45	3.73	4.64	5.01	Kg
Manufacturing energy	813	1204	738	1266	1138	997	Mj
Painting energy	514	514	514	514	514	514	Mj
Use (200,000 km)	1002	775	1504	752	936	1010	Mj
Recycling energy	368	158	95	635	580	424	Mj
Total energy	2697	2651	2851	3167	3168	2945	Mj

Source: IKP, Stuttgart

assessment, reflecting the effect of the weight of the component on fuel consumption.

Like all tools, the use of LCA always requires an awareness of the context: for example, emissions within a closed environment where there is potential for controlling and removing them are far less critical than the same emissions in an uncontrollable environment. This is well illustrated by an LCA study made by BP into the impacts of both high- and low-solvent coatings, both of which it manufactures. The results showed that under many circumstances the energy use and emissions from using low-solvent coatings did not show any significant overall environmental benefits over high-solvent coatings. Indeed, switching to water-based coatings did not always enable a company to reduce its VOC emissions to allowable levels, in which case thermal oxidation would be needed to destroy the emitted VOCs; this, in turn, required significant energy use because of the high content of water vapour and low calorific value of emissions from low-solvent coatings. On the other hand, a similar system of thermal oxidation in a factory using high-solvent coatings often enabled a net reduction in energy consumption because of the high calorific value of traditional solvents, so enabling the factory to recover energy. BP's conclusion was that, for uses such as vehicle manufacture – where the toxic pollutants from the finished product would generally be dispersed in the open air – there was little to choose between the two kinds of coating; but where the end use was more contained – as in a building – there were significant benefits for water-based decorative coatings, as these minimised the risks of harm from air pollution.

Designers also need to be aware of the risk that LCA can inhibit radical thinking. LCA is usually used to look at a product, not at how a particular need might be met in a more environmentally-

---

Box 6.1 LCA in the clothing industry

The Danish clothing manufacturer Novotex was founded in 1983 with nine employee shareholders; ten years later its annual turnover had reached $18 million. Novotex carries out an LCA of each stage of production and rates its products on a scale of 0 to 100 in terms of environmental value, 100 being an unattainable wholly Green product. This has led it to concentrate environmental performance improvement on some key areas. For example, it is increasingly buying cotton that is organically grown, without pesticides, defoliants or artificial fertilisers. In manufacture, only water soluble dyes are used, with hydrogen peroxide being chosen as the bleaching agent to eliminate chlorides. Dyeing is in fully-enclosed high pressure jet machines thus reducing water consumption by 50 per cent and avoiding all air pollution. New cleaning processes have cut the use of heated water by two-thirds while the drying machines recycle 75 per cent of the hot air used.

---

benign way. Transport is an obvious example. An LCA-led approach will look only at how the design of a car can be improved, not at whether a public transport system might be preferable or whether car use can be significantly contained by the extension of information technologies. Indeed, taken at face value, an LCA might indicate some false priorities: for example, the manufacture of computers requires large volumes of hazardous chemicals and solvents and the heavy metals used in the wiring, solder and screens are a significant contributor to heavy metals in the waste stream, all of which would show up as disadvantages in an LCA; yet computers can reduce the need for paper, minimise travel and fuel use, and substantially improve the efficiency of all kinds of activity.

Within these limitations, LCA is a valuable tool in making design choices. It can identify the key areas of concern; it can indicate the most likely routes for improvement; and it can provide quantitative information on the differences between design alternatives.

Lifecycle analysis in practice

Carrying out an LCA may at first sight appear a daunting task, not least because designers usually have little experience of obtaining or using the necessary data on emissions from materials, processes and the use of the product. Fortunately, such information is becoming more readily available, with many materials manufacturers now able to provide at least some of the necessary information.

Earlier in this chapter I described the usefulness of making an initial assessment of where a particular product falls in the hierarchy of environmental importance and, consequently, how much attention needs to be paid to designing to minimise environmental damage. For products that are relatively low down this hierarchy, it is probably unnecessary for the design team to do anything more than a quick check on the use of hazardous substances or rare resources; after this, normal design considerations of maximising the efficient use of materials and so on should cover any real environmental concerns.

An example of an LCA of a product category some way down the hierarchy indicates the kinds of issues the design team should seek to identify. This was a generic study of sofas carried out in 1991 by the Swedish Environmental Research Institute which showed three areas of design interest, two of which could probably have been predicted by any designer, while the third is only obvious from a wider perspective than that of conventional design concerns. One of the two more obvious conclusions was the importance of materials selection, as their production causes considerably larger impacts than the manufacture of the sofa itself. The second readily apparent conclusion is that attention needs to be paid to the selection of paints and glues, both of which can give off toxic emissions during manufacture and (possibly more importantly, as the factory environment can be controlled) in the home. But this LCA also identified transport – both in conveying materials and components and delivering the final product – as a major component of the environmental impacts of a sofa, indicating that the design team should perhaps pay some attention to minimising the space occupied by the finished product in the delivery vehicle. With this guidance, a sofa designer may choose to do a limited LCA of materials, glues and finishes, although the last two may simply need a check to avoid high-solvent finishes and glues.

LCA software

For products higher up the hierarchy, designers should consider utilising the LCA computer software that is becoming available. Some programs are pre-loaded with large quantities of environmental impact data so that virtually all the design team has to do is to feed in the information on the types and quantities of materials, energy consumption and manufacturing processes for a particular product or component and the software will work out the impacts and present the results in tabular or graphical form. However, databases can be purchased separately, which has the advantage that the ones most appropriate for the particular user can be selected.

When choosing such software, there are some basic features that are essential:

■ How easy is it to input design information?
■ Are the LCA results presented in a relevant and comprehensible form? How easy is it to compare the impacts of alternative designs?
■ Can the user weight the importance of different environmental

---

Box 6.2 **Keeping up to date with performance changes**

The environmental performance of materials, processes and energy sources can change rapidly and it is important for designers to ensure that they are using current data. One example of the speed of change is shown by the improvement made by the manufacturer of the UK's top-selling 'Conqueror' range of paper: it cut water consumption by 45 per cent and material loss by 50 per cent in just four years.

---

impacts and can the software then produce a weighted aggregate figure for total impact?

- Does the software allow for easy aggregation of results from different components so that the impacts of a complete product can be built up without re-entering information?
- How comprehensive are the available databases and do they cover the materials, energy sources and manufacturing processes that you are likely to need? Do they include information about recycling options?
- Are the information databases sufficiently relevant to the design projects to which they are applied? For example, are the electricity assumptions close enough to the type of generating source ratios of the country in which the products are to be manufactured or used? Is data for both virgin and recycled sources of the same material provided?
- Can the user easily alter or add to the databases (this can, of course, help overcome the problems referred to above)?
- Is the software supplier likely to update or enhance the databases in the future?

Potential users also need to check the usual software criteria of compatibility with other programs – for example, if materials information can be fed directly from a CAD program into the LCA software, this is obviously advantageous; if not, both may translate into another common format (Excel, for instance) to facilitate information exchange.

Weighting impacts

In the above checklist I have included the ability to weight different kinds of environmental impact. This introduces a key element in the use of LCA, for weighting different types of impact may provide the only way in which the problem of making judgements can be overcome. Sometimes this weighting can be done intuitively: the emission of a relatively small quantity of a highly toxic substance into a closed environment is almost always worse than dumping a much larger quantity of an inert substance into a landfill site. For other products, some of the criteria may be set by statutory or voluntary regulation and one of the purposes of the LCA is to check that these criteria are being met. In other cases, the decisions about the weighting to be given to different criteria may have to be made by the product development team in the light of their own knowledge of the market, the local circumstances, and their own evaluation of the importance of each.

The relevance, reliability and comprehensiveness of the databases are, of course, critical. Before purchasing a database, it is worth investigating whether using a consultant to build up a tailor-made database for the specific use might be a better option than buying a ready-made product.

The range of LCA software that is commercially available is growing rapidly. In order to illustrate the potential benefits for designers, I will describe briefly three that are, at the time of writing, already reasonably well-established.

PIRA International introduced one of the first LCA software systems, PEMS, the development of which was funded jointly by the UK government and the packaging industry. PEMS is capable of conducting an LCA of any product, process or activity. Four databases are included, covering materials, transportation, energy and waste management. The program, while still biased in its databases towards the packaging industry, is worth evaluating for other purposes, especially where issues such as transportation and waste are paramount. A cut down version called EcoAssessor is also available which can compile an environmental impacts burden summary from a simple flow diagram. These programs have the benefit for UK users of offering UK-based databases; PEMS itself is available in either IBM or Mac format, while EcoAssessor is available only in IBM format; both require Excel 5.

The other two are available only in IBM format but have the advantage of being available for initial evaluation in demonstration form free. The first of these, 'LCA Inventory Tool', has been developed by the Swedish company Chalmers Industriteknik and is especially relevant for process design. It is supplied complete with databases holding basic energy and emission data and is based on building up 'cards' for each stage of the lifecycle: these are developed into a flow chart, with the individual impact totals being aggregated as needed and displayed in bar chart form. One of the strengths of the system is that reference text can be added to all data fields, thus facilitating structured documentation that may be needed to meet the requirements of BS 7750 or the EU EMAS scheme.

The third program is 'SimaPro' from the Dutch company PRé Consultants. It comes in two versions, one intended for in-depth analysis and the second – probably of most interest to designers – focusing on the interpretation of results. As well as coming with its own up-to-date databases on materials, processing, transport, energy and waste management, third party databases are being developed for use with 'SimaPro', the first of which will focus on building materials. This program may be the most attractive for industrial designers, as it is somewhat more graphical than the others. Such programs cost between £750 and £2,000 at 1995 prices.

These three programs largely meet the criteria suggested in the checklist above. However, developments in this field are rapid and anyone considering the purchase of LCA software should not take the mention of these three products as being in any way a shortlist. What these examples do show is that the problems of using LCA as a design tool in any meaningful way have been overcome.

Other design tools

There are other computer-based tools being developed to help with other aspects of environmental product development too. Again simply as an illustration I will mention three programs being developed by the Fraunhofer-Institute for Manufacturing Engineering and Automation in Stuttgart. 'RONDA' is a recycling-oriented system that helps to analyse information about a design by analysing databases created by the manufacturer. 'RECREATION' is a database which contains significant information about all suitable recycling processes and their suppliers. Finally, 'RECOVERY' helps to find the most economical strategy for recycling a product. All three of these programs have been designed to work with CAD systems.

It seems likely that the integration of such systems – including LCA programs – into conventional CAD systems will be a feature of future developments.

7 Managing environmental product development

■ Introduction ■ Corporate objectives ■ Product strategy and corporate objectives ■ Information links ■ Procedures for managing the design process ■ Monitoring results ■ Measuring environmental performance ■ Preparing the design team

---

Introduction

Successful product development must, of course, be planned, resourced, monitored and managed. This applies as much to a company's overall design strategy as to an individual design project.

Where a company is operating within the European Union's Ecomanagement and Audit Scheme (EMAS) or BS 7750 *Environmental Management Systems*, these will provide some basic parameters within which the product development team will operate. Most importantly, their adoption will signify a commitment by top management that the company takes environmental considerations seriously throughout its operations.

There is another British Standard to take into account here. Introduced in 1990, BS 7000 provides a *Guide to Managing Product Design*. It is perhaps most valuable in the context of this book in providing a clear outline of the responsibilities of senior managers in relation to the design function. The following is a checklist extrapolated from BS 7000:

■ Have the corporate objectives for the design function been properly defined and, thereafter, periodically reviewed?
■ Are these corporate objectives understood by all involved and have they inspired enthusiasm?
■ Is the company's product strategy compatible with its corporate objectives?
■ Have sufficient resources been provided to match the product strategy?
■ Are procedures in place to ensure that up-to-date information about market requirements is available to the design team?
■ Are the collaborative, information and evaluation links between the design team and other parts of the business operating properly?
■ Are the organisational policies and procedures for managing the design process adequate?
■ Is there a sincere and visible corporate commitment to high standards of product design?
■ Are achievement and expenditure being monitored against time?
■ Are results being properly evaluated and is this evaluation being communicated to all concerned?

I will take these points in turn and explain their particular relevance to Green product development.

Corporate objectives

Defining the corporate objectives for the design function is especially important in an environmental context, as this is a new dimension for many companies and designers and the goals therefore need careful thought. Most importantly, the company needs to decide at Board level why it is asking its design team to take account of environmental issues. Is it simply to comply with current and imminent regulations? Is the company seeking to use environmentally-sound design as a positive competitive weapon to prise open new markets? Does the Board envisage a shift to new technologies in manufacture or in the product? Do environmental driving forces suggest a switch to new product areas altogether, perhaps because of changing lifestyles or increased customer expectations? Is it likely that new legal or standards requirements will present opportunities or challenges?

One example of a company that has rethought its strategy in the light of environmental influences on its business is Walki-Pak, part of the Finland-based international paper corporation United Paper Mills. Table 7.1 indicates the changes.

So important are the product plan and the design brief that these should be subject to approval by senior executives. In particular, they should ensure that these all-important stages both reflect forecast market needs and are in harmony with the company's long-term product strategy. After all, if the brief is deficient the resulting product will be deficient too, thus damaging the company's future performance and its ability to meet its targets.

Tiers of product planning

For most companies, three tiers of product planning are desirable. The first is a long-term product strategy, setting out the general direction in which the company's product ranges will develop in order to meet corporate objectives. Then there is a need for a shorter-term product plan that identifies specific new product needs. Finally, the brief for every new product must not

Table 7.1 **Environmental management paradigms (Walki-Pak in the 1980s and currently)**

Dimension/paradigm	Former (1980s) paradigm: 'Traditional management'	Current paradigm: 'Environment-related management'
Concept of product	Corrugated cardboard box	Corrugated cardboard box as part of the product lifecycle from raw material to disposal
Industry	Packaging industry is a growth industry	Packaging is not likely to increase in Western countries
Competitive advantage	Reasonably priced corrugated board of high quality	Managing the environmental aspect of company activities: using recycled fibre as raw material and managing the collection of corrugated board
Relationship between the product and the environment	Corrugated board is environment friendly because it is made with renewable resources; it is biodegradable and its manufacture does not pollute	Packaging and packaging waste cause environmental problems
View of economy and nature	Environmental protection only creates additional costs	Interdependence of economy and ecology Environmental consciousness and sound business practice are not mutually exclusive
Parties responsible for the environment	Environmental protection is a task for government officials and legislators	Business must take part in solving environmental problems
Environmental policy and management systems	Environmental concerns are extra-business concerns (exogenous)	Environmental considerations are a part of business and product policy decisions

Source: 'Environmental Issues in Product Development Process' (paper written for *Business Ethics Quarterly* by Minna Halme of the University of Tampere, Finland)

only be in harmony with the other two tiers, but must also provide all the information and management guidance necessary to enable the product to be developed and launched successfully.

It is important that objectives are set for a period that is long enough to guide the design team. It should certainly extend beyond a single product and look to a related family of products in order to facilitate evolutionary improvements in response to accelerating technological, regulatory and market changes. For example, a company may decide to penetrate a new market with a product at the top of the performance/price range that makes a special feature of environmental performance – perhaps in terms of outstanding energy efficiency – and then use this to expand market share with lower-priced versions. Obviously, the design team needs to be aware of these objectives before it begins work on the market entry design so as to minimise development costs and time for the second generation version.

With environmental issues still in their infancy, it is essential regularly to review the design team's objectives; this should in any case be normal practice, for companies need to be continually aware of changes in their markets and developments by their competitors.

Box 7.1 Nissan, Honda and Mazda adopt different corporate design strategies

The three major Japanese car manufacturers are responding to pressures for cleaner vehicles in distinctive ways.

Nissan is pursuing an incremental strategy, aiming to achieve substantial improvement in performance through the cumulative effects of many small improvements.

Honda has concentrated on developing the lean-burn engine, arguing that its intrinsically better fuel combustion both reduces pollution and improves efficiency. This strategy was being followed by companies elsewhere – notably Ford and Rover in the UK – however, they dropped it when catalytic converters (CATs) were made mandatory, as it was thought that CATs and lean-burn technology were incompatible. Honda's persistence now seems likely to pay off, as one of its rivals (Mazda) has developed a CAT that will work with lean-burn engines.

Mazda itself has adopted the most radical strategy, inspired by its adoption of the Wankel rotary engine technology. Mazda aims to switch from petrol to non-polluting hydrogen as a fuel, believing that the rotary engine makes hydrogen-powered vehicles economically and technically feasible. The company has already demonstrated a prototype.

Of course, corporate objectives are useless unless they are understood by everyone involved in product development. This is especially important in relation to environmental objectives, again partly because the field is so new but also because there are likely to be some staff who view the subject with some suspicion, either because they do not understand the driving forces or because they are unsure of their own ability to deal with the issues. So handing down objectives from on high will not be effective. A well thought out communications and training strategy is essential.

If a company already has in place an effective Total Quality Management (TQM) philosophy, then adding in the environmental dimension should be comparatively easy since the objectives are wholly compatible. W. Edwards Deming – who devised the TQM approach some 50 years ago – listed as some of the objectives: a commitment to constant improvement; a philosophy of zero errors or defects; an understanding of consumer–supplier relationships; and an assessment of total cost, not economic price alone, all of which are fundamental to environmentally-responsible design too.

Product strategy and corporate objectives

It is also important to check that the company's product strategy is compatible with its corporate objectives. In particular, will the new-product development programme deliver the market share and rate of return needed for the company to achieve the correct combination of growth and profitability to satisfy short-term funding needs and secure long-term growth?

Investing in design costs money. And the Open University research quoted in Chapter 3 suggests that investing in Green design tends to be more resource-demanding than ordinary design projects, probably because it tends to demand a greater degree of innovation. In the past, companies in much of the English-speaking world have used these costs as an excuse to cut back on product development in times of recession, which has been a prime cause of the failure of many such companies to survive when the good times return. For they, unlike their German and Japanese counterparts, have failed to understand that, at the end of recession, many customers will be looking for the best-performing products, not the cheapest, so a company trying to sell elderly designs in such circumstances will suffer badly. As the Open University research demonstrated, despite the greater resources needed, investing in Green design tends to be more rewarding even than investing in standard design projects.

Minimising commercial risk

Another point needs stressing here. Under-resourcing design is a false economy. While investing in design has the potential for improving almost every competitively-sensitive aspect of a product, it is also comparatively inexpensive and risk-free. The management consultancy, McKinsey & Co. carried out a study in 1990 that compared the sensitivity of profits over the life of a product with three potential problems: delayed launch; too high production costs; and an overrun of development costs. Assuming a 20 per cent market growth rate, a 12 per cent annual price erosion and a product life of five years, McKinsey found that a development cost overrun of 50 per cent would reduce after-tax profits by just 3.5 per cent. But a 9 per cent overshoot in production costs reduced profits by 22 per cent, and missing the launch date by six months cost 33 per cent of the profits of the project.

If a company decides that environmental issues are important in its product development strategy, then it must make sure that the development team is properly resourced to cope with this new demand. Resources may include the use of external consultancy expertise, the purchase of computer software, training, and the setting up of systems to enable the designers to link in with other information sources. There is also likely to be a need to devote time to ensuring that suppliers and subcontractors can meet the new requirements.

Information links

Designers cannot operate in isolation. It has long been recognised that a characteristic of successful product design is the integration of the design process with all other parts of the business, with effective two-way communication being the norm. This must start right at the beginning, with the product planning and preparation of the design brief. These will guide the whole design process and so must be developed in collaboration with the designers to ensure the full analysis and understanding of the requirements of the ultimate customer. Green concerns emphasise the importance of these stages, for customers, too, may be new to this particular scene and the designers will need to be aware of how customers' preferences are likely to develop.

The role of design in minimising environmental impact during the manufacturing stage of a product's life underscores the need for close collaboration with those involved in manufacture, assembly and testing. This is necessary not just to ensure that a design is economic to manufacture, but also to short-circuit any potential environmental problems by, for example, designing for a less polluting process. This collaboration must extend to suppliers and subcontractors too, especially if the company is operating formal procedures under BS 7750 or EMAS.

Feedback

Systems to ensure feedback to the design team from those involved with the product after it leaves the factory – purchasers, operators, service engineers – is always important, providing essential information for the design of second generation products. In the environmental context, such feedback should include checks on how the product is actually used to see if the environmental benefits designed in are being achieved in practice. The feedback system should extend, where possible, to monitoring how the product is disposed of at the end of its life, so that next-generation designs can simplify recycling or remanufacture or ensure safe disposal.

Of course, this last may merely be completing the circle. For where a company is setting up a specific disposal system – such as the collect and recycle strategies that are being developed by some industry responsibility groups – then the designers need to liaise at the first design stage with those who will be responsible for disposal in order to minimise end-of-life costs.

Information needs go beyond the product. The product development team needs to keep up to date with impending legislation, with technical developments, and with what competitors are doing. This, of course, should be standard practice, irrespective of environmental considerations. The openness of Japanese companies has given them a huge advantage in this, for the Japanese custom of collaborating with government agencies, trade associations and even direct competitors means that information and best practice disseminates rapidly. It may be that the producer responsibility groups now being set up in the UK and elsewhere in reaction to the environmental challenge will help to make such co-operation more acceptable in the West.

Procedures for managing the design process

The basic principles for managing product development are the same as for managing any other activity and anyone seeking sound guidance need look no further than BS 7000. Nevertheless, there are three points worth emphasising here, as they are especially relevant to environmentally-aware product development.

The first is the importance of time. Product development is a competitive process, with manufacturers leap-frogging each other in producing improved products. Beating the opposition to the marketplace with an innovation has two key advantages: it gains attention for the product in a way that is just not available to the runner-up and, possibly more importantly, it maximises the time for making sales and profits before the next-generation product comes along to take the market

The objective of minimising development times can, however, be put at some risk when a design team is asked to take environmental considerations into account for the first time, because the learning process can be quite difficult – the Open University study quoted earlier found that Green design projects tended to take longer to come to fruition than standard projects. This risk can be at least partially overcome by giving the product development team time to consider and prepare for the environmental implications of a project in advance of setting the detailed design brief and by ensuring that the key environmental issues are clearly identified at the conceptual stages of the project.

The second point is linked to the first and is already well accepted in many companies: this is the need for flat organisational structures and the maximum flexibility and effectiveness in communications. This is critical if environmental targets are to be met in a reasonable timescale, for the knock-on effects of early design decisions affect not just the economy of manufacture and the performance of the product, but also the environmental impacts at the end of its life.

Finally, the management structure must encourage innovation and lateral thinking. Environmental issues present opportunities for entirely novel ways of achieving success. The product development team – and anyone else who can contribute ideas – should be given the opportunity at the concept stage to consider alternative ways of providing the service needed by the customer. Product development teams can, almost by definition, become obsessed by product improvement and fail to find the time to stand back and ask if this is really the best approach. Once again, the TQM philosophy of focusing on satisfying customer needs fits in well with the needs of environmental product development.

Monitoring results

Monitoring and evaluating results are essential to the effective management of any activity. As with all design projects, it is

---

***Box 7.2* Bell Atlantic benefits from innovation**

Innovative thinking is a key to competitiveness in the environmental field. One company that has benefited is the American telephone company Bell Atlantic, which has experimented with replacing paper telephone directories with CD-I players. This has proved to save money as well as trees. Each disc contains 1.6 million numbers and costs $2.5 compared with $5 for a paper directory.

important at the beginning of the project to fix set points at which the project will be reviewed to ensure that costs, timescales, specifications and so on are on target. These reviews must be honest and open and it is essential that the results – good or bad – are communicated to all concerned.

From the point of view of environmental performance, lifecycle analysis will indicate whether the targets set at the beginning of the project for environmental impact are being achieved. However, for products where significant impacts come in the use phase of the product's life, it is important to ensure that the user-interface works in the way intended by the designers. For such products, consumer-testing should be carried out during development to check the percentage of users who adopt the desired behaviour.

Measuring and monitoring has a wider purpose in the context of the increasing need for companies to be publicly accountable for their environmental performance. The next section therefore looks at the wider issues of measuring environmental performance.

Measuring environmental performance

There are many approaches to measuring environmental performance, including:

■ Impact measures tracking the environmental consequences of business activities.
■ Risk measures assessing the likelihood and consequences of environmentally harmful events.
■ Emissions/wastes measures tracking the mass or volumes of emissions to air, soil, water and solid waste disposal.
■ Input measures focusing on the effectiveness of environment-

related business processes within the company.

- Resource measures recording consumption of resources.
- Efficiency measures monitoring wastage in the use of energy and materials.
- Customer measures concerned with the satisfaction and behaviour of customers.
- Financial measures assessing the costs and benefits of environment-related actions.

Peter James and Martin Bennett of the Ashridge Management Research Group have defined six different approaches (see Table 7.2).[1] They point out that measures can be manipulated in two ways. 'Normalised' measures relate data in two dimensions –

Table 7.2 **Approaches to environmental performance measurement**

Approach	Orientation	Drivers	Measurement focus	Metrics
Production	Engineering	Efficiency	Mass/energy balance	Efficiency Financial Resources
Auditing	Legalistic	Compliance	Management systems Risks Violations	Emissions/waste Input Risk
Ecological	Scientific	Impacts	Lifecycle analysis Impact assessment	Emissions/waste Impacts Resources
Accounting	Reporting	Costs Accountability	Liabilities Impacts on society	Financial Emissions/waste (for reporting)
Economic	Welfare	Externalities	Shadow pricing	Financial
Quality	Continuous improvement	Pollution Prevention Customers (Internal/external)	Waste Generation/emissions Cost of Quality	Customer Efficiency Emissions/waste Financial Input Normalisation Resources

Source: Peter James and Martin Bennett (1994) *Financial Dimensions of Environmental Performance: Developments in Environment-related Management Accounting* published by the Ashridge Management Research Group

energy consumption per tonne of output, for example – while 'aggregate' measures convert data in multiple dimensions into a single dimension by, for instance, assigning a monetary value to the data or creating a qualitative scoring system.

There are no absolute rules on what constitutes good performance; this depends ultimately on the values and priorities of individual companies and the relevant audiences. Financial stakeholders demand reassurance that their investments and loans are not at risk from poor environmental performance; insurers, regulatory bodies and so on want to know that the company is doing everything it can to minimise environmental harm; buyers seeking to purchase goods and services from environmentally-responsible suppliers need proof; and companies need to measure performance to give their own staff clear directions.

Individual companies need to decide why and what they are measuring, whether within the formal framework of EMAS or BS 7750 or not. Once these decisions have been taken, appropriate measures and targets should be set for the product development team, both in the short term and the long term.

Preparing the design team

For most designers, environmental considerations present an entirely new challenge. Unless they have qualified very recently, their training is unlikely to have included the subject: there are comparatively few genuine Green exemplars, and there has been controversy and confusion over some of the approaches that have been taken to tackling the issues. Before embarking on a detailed examination of the different elements of environmental product development, it is therefore worth looking briefly at the problems likely to confront designers in this field.

Box 7.3 **Sustainable product development – the Philips experience**

Philips Consumer Electronics has been addressing general environmental issues for some 25 years but only began to look at environmentally-oriented product development comparatively recently. The company's basic objective is sustainable product development, which it defines as 'production, use and end-of-life of products that does not hamper the well-being of future generations'. Philips started to analyse the cradle-to-grave environmental impacts of products in the late 1980s, concentrating on the use of resources and end-of-life re-use in any form. The company has now developed an environmental design manual that forms the basis of moves towards sustainable product development. The manual provides the general background and information on environmental issues relevant to the consumer electronics industry and surveys and consolidates information on environmental directives and recommendations. These are applied globally, irrespective of the location of either the development or manufacturing site.

The manual covers environmental policy and organisation; the release status of components and materials; energy consumption; end-of-life; packaging; marking, labelling and customer information; purchasing; production operations; and environmental design evaluation. Produced by a small group of environmental specialists within the Philips Product Division, the manual is being implemented by the same team with support from environmental managers within the company's business groups. Training courses are held to launch implementation at each site, with specified products being used to act as a carrier for the message. This introductory phase is followed by product improvement based on lifecycle assessment, with full compliance with the manual following.

From this experience, Philips suggests that there are three critical factors in success: the integration of environmental considerations into procedures, practice and mind-sets; insight into cost consequences; and decisions on how priorities are set.

Environmental product development requires some fundamental changes in approach by designers. Most important is the concept of product stewardship. Traditionally, designers have confined their work to considerations affecting just a part of the lifecycle of a product: meeting the needs of the user and ensuring that a product can be manufactured efficiently have been the key aims. Environmental product development extends these considerations to the whole life of the product, from the effects of the acquisition of the raw materials to what happens to the product when its useful life ends.

Ecological responsibilities

The designer's responsibilities are extended in another dimension too. Designers have long had a responsibility for the direct health and safety consequences of their work, ranging from trying to minimise injuries in car accidents to ensuring correct task lighting to avoid eye damage. Now those responsibilities are extended to the welfare of the global ecology. The Kew Gardens' bus (Figure 7.1) illustrates how one design team has fulfilled its joint environmental and social responsibilities.

Figure 7.1 **Clean bus for Kew**

People with difficulty walking can use a specially-designed clean bus when they visit the Royal Botanical Gardens at Kew in London. Designed by Sir Norman Foster and Partners, the electric vehicle is powered partly by batteries and partly by solar power, the latter providing up to a third of the necessary energy on sunny days. With large windows that can be fully opened to provide passengers with something of the smell and sounds – as well as the sights – of the Gardens, the bus also features an air suspension system that enables the chassis to be lowered to ground level so that people in wheelchairs can easily enter and exit. The bus is designed to operate only within the grounds of Kew Gardens and has a range of just 12 km between battery recharging; the maximum load is 18 passengers and the top speed is 12 mph. (Photograph by Richard Davies.)

These extended responsibilities are being formally recognised by designers' professional bodies. In 1991, the British Chartered Society of Designers introduced a new Code of Conduct that included a clause requiring its members to

> have due regard to the effect of their work and endeavour that it may cause as little harm as possible either directly or indirectly to the ecology or environment, including living creatures; endangered species of plant or fauna; the atmosphere, rivers and seas. Members shall wherever possible encourage the conservation of energy and the recycling of used products, packaging and materials.

The UK Engineering Council has published a Code of Professional Practice on *Engineers and the Environment*, the main points of which include a duty to work to enhance the quality of the environment; to make systematic reviews on environmental issues; to balance economic, environmental and social benefits; and to keep up to date by seeking education and training.

In the United States, the Industrial Designers Society of America has approved some Principles of Ecological Design that call for designers to reduce the use of natural resources; select ecologically appropriate materials; choose environmentally safe processes; and design for the life of the product.

Unsurprisingly, there is a notable difference of emphasis in approach between engineering and industrial designers. Being science-based, engineering designers are generally better equipped to analyse the often complex technical factors involved in making choices to reduce environmental impacts. In its booklet *Guidelines on Environmental Issues*, the UK Engineering Council states that

Engineers can bring many 'objective' measures to assist in choices of technology and decisions which involve complex trade-offs or conflicts of interest, but they will only be able to make a significant contribution to the general debate if their intervention is based on a solid understanding of the integration of broader environmental concerns with the other issues at stake.

Guidelines on Environmental Issues gives as an example of the technical complications the use of catalytic converters in cars, concluding that

If the full lifecycle of the catalytic converter is examined (including the energy required during production and the subsequent recycling of materials and disposal of old converters), and this is added to the reduced efficiency of most engines fitted with a catalytic converter (in some cases up to 10 per cent with a concomitant increase in final fuel consumption), it is clear that for many typical car journeys it is not ideal for reducing pollution levels from cars.

This clearly demonstrates the need for designers to be able to test the validity of accepted wisdom and challenge preconceptions that prove unsupportable.

Lateral thinking

Arts-based industrial designers are well-used to assessing the qualities of different materials and understanding the design potential of different production processes; but where the choice enters new areas – such as comparing the impacts of differing volumes of different types of emission – many industrial designers may find some difficulty in drawing conclusions. But experience shows that the talent that many industrial designers have for side-

Figure 7.2 Safe cycling

Cycling is rising up the agenda of government and local authorities as a way of reducing car use. But families with young children are often unable to cycle once the children grow too big for a child seat, as the dangers of road traffic are too great to risk young children on their own bikes. An innovative solution has come from Islabikes, which has developed a trailerbike for children that attaches to the rear of an adult's machine. The trailer is designed so that the rider can contribute power through a normal pedal and chain mechanism. (Islabikes.)

stepping problems with a completely new solution can be especially valuable in tackling environmental issues. A good example is the way in which industrial designer Stephen Blanchard approached the problem of what to do with one of the most difficult of post-consumer wastes, discarded electric cabling. Instead of attempting to devise ways of stripping the plastic from the copper and then trying to recycle these, Blanchard turned what are usually regarded as problems into a positive advantage. He devised a way of shredding the cable – complete with its mixed colours and copper – and then mixing, heating and pressing it to create decorative panels that exploit the colour variety and occasional glint of copper to produce a smooth decorative board suitable for such non-structural uses as interior claddings, shelving and so on.

Industrial designers also have an ability to tackle the emotional and cultural aspects of product choice and use. This, too, can be of critical importance when trying, for example, to persuade people to keep a product for longer. As Bill Stephenson, Deputy Chairman of the UK development company Bellway told a conference in London at the end of 1994, 'Long life is not necessarily to do with inherent strength but is inspired by something that people want to keep, care for and sustain'.

Avoid preconceptions

Irrespective of design discipline, two further points are worth making here. First, the assessment of environmental impacts is rarely easy and preconceptions are frequently wrong, as was illustrated by the catalytic converter analysis quoted in Box 7.1. This is true even for apparently simple products: many people assume that oil-based plastics are likely to be inherently less environment-friendly than paper products made from a renewable resource. But a German research project has shown conclusively that brown paper bags have a greater environmental impact on all counts than polythene, even assuming that the paper is recycled while the plastic is dumped (see Table 7.3). Another German project indicated that returnable drinks bottles may be less environmentally sound than their throw-away rivals. And a third questioned the efficacy of that icon of many environmentalists, the electric car, finding that replacing the million or so internal combustion-engined vehicles in Cologne with electric-engined alternatives would lead to a 20 per cent rise in net carbon dioxide emissions and an increase in sulphur dioxide. The Engineering Council's *Guidelines on Environmental Issues* is right to warn that perceptions are more likely to be affected by social, economic and political factors than by scientific awareness.

The second point is that the incorporation of environmental factors into product development adds even greater weight to the

Table 7.3 **The environmental burden of 1 million bags**

	Polythene bags	Paper bags
Energy required	580,000 megajoules	1,340,000 megajoules
Sulphur dioxide	198 kg	388 kg
Nitrous oxides	136 kg	204 kg
Hydrocarbons	76 kg	24 kg
Carbon monoxide	20 kg	60 kg
Dust	10 kg	64 kg
Waste water	10 kg	512 kg

Source: German Federal Office of the Environment (1988)

importance of the early stages of the design process. The American Research Council has estimated that 70 per cent of the costs of product development, manufacture and use are determined during the initial design stages; when end-of-life and pollution costs are added into this equation, the importance of getting the initial concept right becomes even greater.

Not only are Green pressures more likely to stimulate the demand for innovation and design than they are to inhibit it, but also the designers' skills in developing and analysing alternative approaches, in selecting the best materials for a specific purpose, in refining details to minimise cost and in ensuring a satisfactory interface between the user and the product are all crucial to achieving a product that minimises environmental damage. Just as vital to successful Green product development are the design skills used in making judgements about the most effective balance between the inevitable conflicts that arise between different aspects of the performance of a product. Designers have nothing to fear from the intrusion of environmental factors into product development: far from inhibiting design or creativity, environmental issues are acting as a catalyst for innovative design.

8 Exploiting design for the environment

■ Introduction ■ Analysing the market ■ The
opportunities ■ Customer loyalty ■ Selling
environmental technology

Introduction

Having developed a product that incorporates environmental
benefits, it is, of course, important to exploit these advantages
commercially. This chapter concentrates on the marketing issues
directly involving the product rather than on the wider
commercial advantages of site or company-wide approval to be
gained from BS 7750 or EMAS.

Analysing the market

The first point to make is that the environmental sophistication of
purchasers varies enormously. In general, professional purchasers
such as architects and those specifying goods and equipment for
large companies are likely to be comparatively environmentally
aware and have some idea of the issues relevant to a particular
product type. The level of awareness and knowledge among the
general public is far more diverse, particularly when looked at
internationally. For instance, consumers in Holland and Germany
generally have more experience of making informed choices on

environmental matters than their counterparts in the UK.

Again, there is considerable variation in what influences different people and organisations in making purchasing decisions. Business purchasers are, for instance, more likely to be influenced by lifetime cost factors than the general public (although even with business purchasers this tends to concentrate on specific aspects rather than making a comprehensive lifetime costing assessment).

However, there are indications of a strong latent desire for more Green information among the public which could – with the right trigger – lead to some rapid changes. For instance, a National Consumer Council survey found that 80 per cent of consumers thought that accurate information about product life expectancy was essential or very important; 40 per cent thought that the information provided by manufacturers and retailers was poor or very poor.[1]

Where the design team has sought environmental advantage through innovation, the implications for marketing need especially careful analysis. Novelty can be a curse or a blessing. In some market sectors, it is almost a prerequisite for success: children buying electronic games look not just for a new game but insist on using the latest technology. But consumer resistance to new ways of carrying out such basic tasks as washing clothes is likely to be high: how would UK consumers take to the idea of soaking clothes in a cold wash overnight instead of using a hot wash? Yet this is how many families in Canada and Japan carry out their family washing.

The opportunities

Defining the selling points of the product that are most

appropriate to each market are – as always – the key to the successful marketing of Green products. However, there are a number of factors specific to marketing in the environmental context. Perhaps the first is a warning: the powerful and vigilant environmental lobby means that any Green claims made for a product or service are likely to be scrutinised closely and criticised loudly if they cannot be justified with firm evidence. The legal constraints on unjustified claims are being tightened too. The UK government, for instance, announced in 1994 that it intended to amend the Trade Descriptions Act to stop the abuse of environmental claims, particularly regarding descriptions of products as recycled or recyclable; an Environmental Claims Bill began its Parliamentary progress in 1995.

On the positive side, there is a strong desire on the part of many retailers and corporate purchasers to be seen to be Green. The media, too, are often attracted by a story with a Green slant. So the opportunities for using Green product features to gain positive publicity and marketing advantages can be significant. For some products – especially office goods – specialist suppliers have appeared dedicated to providing only environmentally-designed merchandise and thus offering manufacturers of such items with a direct line to buyers seeking Green credentials.

Public relations is especially important where the design of the product requires some readjustment in attitude on the part of the prospective purchaser. Taking as an example the use of a washing machine featuring a long, overnight cold wash programme, this would be unlikely to sell well in the UK without a considerable educational programme aimed at convincing the public that it performed effectively and that it made significant savings in energy costs and pollution. Support from retailers and the media would be crucial and, because of the novelty, available.

Box 8.1 **Information sells**

The retail group B&Q has tried a number of experiments to see if raising the profile of the environmental issues of a particular product type would have much effect on sales. In one case, a local school was provided with peat and peat-free growing bags to do their own trials on plant growth; in another, customers seen buying peat-based products were approached by staff, who explained the issue. B&Q's sales figures backed up anecdotal evidence of a direct correlation between buying decisions and information about relevant environmental issues.

Endorsement from independent environmental organisations would be likely too but would need careful judgement; after all, the public still tends to attribute a beards-and-sandals image to Green enthusiasts and this is hardly the image wanted by a washing machine manufacturer. Detergent and clothing manufacturers would probably need to be brought into the campaign to give the system credibility.

It is worth noting that independent environmental information centres are beginning to be provided in some countries, including the UK and Eire. Usually financed by local authorities or central government, these have a dual role of providing general educational information about the environment and specific assistance for people wanting advice on recycling, home insulation and so on. Many of these centres are willing to help promote products with proven environmental benefits and some may be prepared to help with publicity campaigns aimed at promoting innovative Green products.

Labelling

Where there is an independent environmental labelling scheme for the particular product area, this may be all that is needed to indicate official endorsement of a product's Green credentials.

Box 8.2 **Learning from Shell's disaster**

The speed with which a company can lose its environmental reputation through public relations and strategic misjudgements was illustrated by the experience of Shell in 1995. Shell had built an enviable reputation over many years with a programme that included long-term extensive advertising explaining how it was fulfilling its environmental responsibilities and by such activities as sponsorship of a high-profile environmental awards scheme. All this disintegrated when the company's decision to dump its defunct 14,000 tonne Brent Spar gas platform at the bottom of the Atlantic was challenged by Greenpeace in a high-profile and well-organised media campaign. Within a few days, German motorists were boycotting Shell petrol stations, the German Chancellor was censoring Shell for its environmental irresponsibility, and the UK media was having a field day at Shell's expense. Eventually, Shell was forced into a humiliating climb-down, despite having been backed by the UK government.

The lessons are perhaps not obvious, for Shell's errors had less to do with environmental irresponsibility than with an inability to communicate effectively. Greenpeace had, in fact, got the science wrong: Shell's decision to dump in the deep ocean was almost certainly correct, for the very local and relatively minor pollution would have caused virtually no damage, while land-based disposal involved real hazards (for example, the asbestos in the platform is harmless under water but hazardous when airborne). But Shell never explained the science satisfactorily, allowing Greenpeace to get away with over-hyped claims, some of which Greenpeace later admitted was based on faulty measurements.

Shell also made two strategic errors. First, it decided on dumping at sea as the best option in this particular case without looking at the wider issue of what would happen if everyone started dumping such major structures at sea. It was an almost moral repugnance at treating the sea as a dumping ground that provoked such public anger – and Greenpeace was right to highlight this wider risk. Shell's second error was made more than 20 years earlier, when the Brent Spar was being designed. For Shell had failed to ensure that the platform was designed to facilitate safe disassembly and disposal. That failure cost the company many millions of pounds and its environmental reputation.

The benefits are obvious. Nevertheless, labelling may not be the best – or the only – route for every manufacturer or product.

The first dilemma is for the manufacturer whose product significantly exceeds the standards required by the particular labelling scheme. Simply to use the label may merely bring the product down to the same level as its rivals in the eyes of the consumer. It may be that the label still has to be used – it is independent and its omission may be detrimental if rival products carry it – but it should be backed up with additional point-of-sale and advertising information making clear the superior qualities of this particular product.

Occasionally, a manufacturer may wish deliberately to refrain from taking part in an official labelling scheme. One company that has taken this route is the UK-based retail group, the Body Shop, which has flourished and grown internationally on a reputation for an ethical approach to business. The company withdrew from the group developing the EU Ecolabel on hairsprays because the testing of products on animals was rejected as a disqualification for the Ecolabel. While the EU's arguments that the Ecolabel is concerned with environmental impact and that animal rights is an ethical rather than an environmental issue seem correct, it is also true that the general public tends to associate the two and therefore that the Body Shop's response was reasonable. Although the Body Shop's decision was motivated by its ethical stance, it is fair to point out that it is unlikely that the lack of a label on its hairsprays would damage a company whose success is largely due to its ethical and Green renown; its public stand on the issue of animal rights will simply have reinforced that reputation.

Manufacturers also need to be aware that there can be a danger in making environmental claims even when these are apparently justified. This arises particularly where an entirely different kind of design approach offers notable environmental advantages over the product that is being claimed as beneficial. For example, battery manufacturers have backed claims that their new, mercury-free products are significantly superior to their predecessors with perfectly proper lifecycle assessments. However, disposable batteries as such are extremely wasteful and polluting when compared with the alternative system of rechargeable batteries. No amount of evidence of environmental improvement can offset this basic disadvantage of ordinary batteries. A similar criticism can be made of paper coffee filters, where the development of an unbleached alternative has been proclaimed as Green by their manufacturers. The environmental impacts are, without doubt, less than for bleached filters but the system cannot compete in environmental terms with the alternative of re-usable filters.

Customer loyalty

It is reasonable to assume that a customer who has been influenced to buy a product partly on its environmental performance will take such considerations into account when considering a repeat purchase. So a manufacturer hoping to sell again to that customer must make sure that the environmental advantages are delivered in use and that the Green message is reinforced at every opportunity. The Body Shop is a classic example of how a company has built international commercial success in a highly competitive market area on this basis. In another sector, the leading home care product manufacturer S.C. Johnson has underlined its environmental improvements with packaging highlighting the Green advantage (see Figure 8.1).

In Chapter 5 I stressed the importance of ensuring that the product is designed to ensure that the user can easily achieve the full environmental benefits of a product by, for example, designing the controls and clear 'on-machine' instructions to guide the user to the ideal performance. This, of course, also applies to instruction manuals and – where appropriate – training packages. For complex commercial products, performance

Figure 8.1 **S.C. Johnson stays in front**

Although CFCs had been removed from all domestic aerosol products by the end of 1989, S.C. Johnson – the manufacturer of Europe's best-selling furniture polish brand, 'Pledge' – was concerned that the public retained some suspicion about the environmental-friendliness of aerosols and that butane (used as the replacement for CFCs as the propellant) was not immune from criticism. So, in 1994 and after a considerable research programme, the company moved to the use of compressed air as the propellant. The company ensured that the new Green attributes of 'Pledge' were underlined by a prominent flash on the front of the pack and a more detailed explanatory panel on the back. 'Pledge' retained its market lead without any additional advertising, despite a major advertising campaign from one of its rivals. (S.C. Johnson.)

targets should be indicated clearly and systems suggested for monitoring these. The benefits can be considerable: experience has shown that providing familiarisation training for vehicle drivers to encourage them to gain maximum fuel efficiency can cut fuel costs by 15 per cent or more.

This can be taken further, for example, by providing information and support systems to encourage and assist repair. Some products are used in circumstances that make damage probable and a recognition that repair is likely to be necessary is an essential part of the manufacturer's customer care package. An example is the surfboard, which can be damaged in accidents or by misuse. In this case, the customer brand loyalty is likely to be enhanced by the inclusion with the product of advice on how

---

Box 8.3 AEG makes a simple change

The German domestic appliance manufacturer AEG took a simple step to underline its environmental concerns when it changed the 'Half-load' button on its washing machines into a 'Green' button. Such marketing ploys can only be effective if they are based on genuine environmental advantage, as in this case.

---

to set about repairing any damage that does occur, including information about repair materials and stockists and, perhaps, the provision of a repair kit. The manufacturer's caring image can then be underlined by pointing out the environmental resource advantages of having provided for the extension of the life of the product through repair.

Selling environmental technology

For environmental technology equipment, there is an additional factor to consider. The companies purchasing such equipment are often doing so as part of a wider project aimed at solving a specific problem. For example, the toughening of environmental regulations may require them to install a new waste treatment plant which can comprise not just the main cleaning process equipment but also monitoring devices, materials recovery systems and so on. Increasingly, purchasers are looking for an integrated solution – they do not want the distraction of having to carefully analyse the merits of individual components.

This has led the UK government's Joint Environmental Markets Unit to consider setting up an industry-run organisation to facilitate co-operation between UK manufacturers in order to offer complete package solutions to environmental requirements. In the meantime, companies manufacturing the individual components needed for major environmental projects should consider collaborating with each other in marketing their goods.

In summary, products that have been designed to minimise their environmental impact can offer significant additional marketing opportunities. Taking full advantage of those opportunities requires careful analysis of the markets and the expectations of the audiences to be addressed.

9 Packaging, distribution and the workplace

■ Introduction ■ Packaging ■ Distribution ■ The workplace

Introduction

As has been explained before, a company that wishes to gain a competitive advantage through a positive approach to environmental issues must take a comprehensive approach covering all of its operations. This is, of course, essential to meet the requirements of BS 7750 and EMAS. This chapter looks briefly at the role that can be played by design in improving environmental performance beyond the product itself. In particular, it looks at packaging, transport and building issues.

Packaging

I will begin with packaging, as this is directly related to product development. Packaging has been at the forefront of environmental attention from the early years of Green activism. This is partly because packaging is, by definition, ephemeral and is therefore seen by some as unnecessary and wasteful. Packaging also suffers from the high visibility of litter – much of it discarded packaging – that is all too evident on streets, beaches and elsewhere.

Germany was the first country to take draconian measures to tackle the perceived packaging problem with its 'green dot' scheme whereby manufacturers have to contribute to a fund to pay for the collection of waste packaging for recycling, their products then being marked with a green dot to indicate compliance. By 1994, proponents of the scheme were claiming that it was saving 500,000 tonnes of material a year. But the scheme has been heavily criticised. Within Germany, there are those who argue that the costs of dealing with waste should be added at the primary commodity stage, not the product, so as to create a market for recycled materials by pushing up the price of virgin materials. Outside Germany, the initial effects on the market for recycled materials – paper in particular – were disastrous, as the huge volumes collected were dumped on other European markets. However, this latter problem diminished as the paper industry emerged from slump.

France has a somewhat similar scheme to that in Germany. The 'Return-Mark' scheme is run by AEME – the Agency for the Environment and for Energy Management – under the supervision of the Ministry for the Environment. Manufacturers pay around £2,000 to use the scheme mark, and arrangements can be put in place for the collection and return of the product at the end of its life, usually paid for by adding the cost at the point of sale, although alternatives are allowed.

In 1994 – after lengthy discussion – the European Union introduced a Directive on Packaging Waste. This aims to improve dramatically the re-use of the resources that go into packaging, whether by recycling materials or by incinerating waste packaging for energy recovery. The Directive sets specific recovery targets: by 2001, 50–65 per cent of packaging wastes must be recovered, of which 25–45 per cent must be recycled; in addition, at least

---

Box 9.1 **Better cans**

Steady advances in design have greatly reduced the material used in drinks cans. Since 1988, the average weight of a beer or soft drinks can has been reduced by 10 per cent and a further 20 per cent reduction is being made possible by, for instance, narrowing the end diameter of cans. An increase in the use of recycled steel and aluminium has helped reduce the energy needed to manufacture cans by 40 per cent.

---

15 per cent of each material must be 15 per cent recycled.

In the UK, the 1995 Environment Act sets a target within the Directive of recovering 58 per cent of packaging waste by 2000. Companies within the packaging chain have responded by establishing VALPAK, an industry responsibility group that will develop voluntary systems for meeting the targets.

This may appear to set a clear direction for manufacturers and designers. Designers need to give top priority to ensuring that packaging is easy to recycle, while manufacturers need to work with others in the use, recovery and recycling chain to ensure that recovery is carried out in the most cost-effective manner. However, responsible companies should consider a second environmental priority: minimising packaging. Many would argue that minimisation is a better route to cutting the environmental impacts of packaging than concentrating on recycling, as it cuts resource use at source. However, minimisation does not make any contribution to the EU or UK government targets, which are based entirely on the recovery of a percentage of the resources put into packaging. This is so illogical that the rules may change, although probably not for some considerable time as experience has shown that arriving at a consensus on issues such as this is never rapid, especially when the politicians can claim to have taken action already.

Box 9.2 Minimising the impact of packaging

Vitrex, one of B&Q's suppliers, has redesigned the packaging of its handtools to meet the DIY chain's requirements, with considerable benefits that include:
- Halving the cardboard used in retail packs.
- Using thinner plastic in blister packs and replacing some blister packs with polypropylene mounting clips.
- An increase in the use of post-consumer recycled material and the elimination of all non-water based varnishes.
- The elimination of staples and plastic adhesive tape in transit and display cartons, thus facilitating recycling.

One consequence of the approach taken by the authorities is the likely focusing of effort on packaging that remains within the manufacturer/distributor chain, as this is clearly easier to recover and re-use than packaging that is released into the care of the general public. Gains in this area will, because of the way the targets have been set, offset the need for more difficult and expensive post-consumer waste recovery systems. So manufacturers should be considering setting up systems with those whom they sell, to recover and re-use such packaging, even where this may, in the short run, require investment in the development of returnable and re-usable packaging. Figure 9.1

Box 9.3 Recovering packaging from retailers

Alida Recycling Ltd has invested £5 million in a plant that takes back-of-store and transit waste from retailers, sorts and cleans it, and produces clean polythene pellets ready for re-use in making packaging and rigid products. The collection, recycling and use of the end material are all in place. The environmental benefits are considerable: a lifecycle assessment carried out by Nottingham University Consultants showed that manufacturing virgin polystyrene compared with recycling used three times more energy; produced two and a half times more CO_2; used eight times as much water; produced three times as much SO_2; and twice as much NOx (including all collection and transport elements).

Figure 9.1 **Re-usable bulk packaging systems**

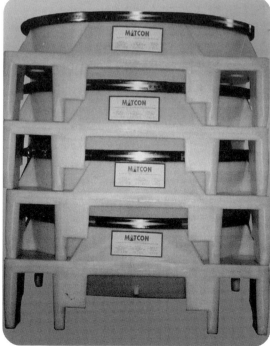

Matcon, an international manufacturer of packaging systems for bulk distribution, introduced a range of re-usable containers for powders and bulk particulates in 1995. Designed to interface with automatic filling and emptying systems, the containers are easy to clean and offer complete containment for the product at every stage to avoid any risk of contamination. (MATCON Ltd.)

shows how one packaging manufacturer has responded to pressures for reusable bulk packaging.

Distribution

Transport – like packaging – is one of the most sensitive of environmental issues. Congestion, concerns about the links between vehicle pollution and asthma and other health problems, and the substantial and increasing share of global warming emissions attributed to transport, combine to make efficient transport systems a necessity. Improved vehicle design – ranging from new engine management and pollution control systems to wind deflectors to improved vehicle aerodynamics and vehicle controls that encourage efficient driver behaviour – is enhancing fuel efficiency. Product manufacturers can play a part too.

One consideration for manufacturers' design teams is to ensure that the product and its packaging are designed to maximise the number of units that can be loaded into a vehicle. When Hoover was designing its 'New Wave' washing machine (see Box 1.1 page 4) it also replaced part of its lorry fleet; by designing the vehicle bodywork specifically for the washing machine, the company increased its capacity by 20 per cent, thus reducing both costs and pollution. In some cases, it may be worth examining whether significant transport savings can be made by moving the product broken-down into subassemblies or – for products distributed world-wide – even by manufacturing bulky fabrications locally. Transport savings may also be made by specifying components and supplies from a limited number of suppliers, as this is likely to result in fewer delivery journeys.

Furniture manufacturers have long recognised the benefits of minimising the bulk of their products during transport by delivering in 'knock-down' form wherever possible. In the early days, this led to considerable resentment from customers faced with complex home-assembly assisted by instruction manuals that were often confusing or inadequate. Nowadays, most knock-down furniture has been carefully designed for easy assembly, overcoming consumer resistance.

Transport and related packaging costs can sometimes outweigh the advantages of centralised production. For instance, the centralisation of production in the highly price-competitive market for bread is now proving to be of doubtful economic value. During the 1970s and 1980s, many small bakeries around the UK closed in the face of competition from large bakeries. However, these large bakeries are now citing the rising cost of transport and plastics packaging to justify price rises. Ironically, plastics wrappers are needed only because factory-produced bread becomes stale much more quickly than traditionally-baked bread.

In many instances, such considerations are likely to be something of a side issue, for the transport savings are likely to be minor compared with other commercial considerations. However, the balance is likely to swing somewhat in the future, as there is little doubt that the costs of transport will rise quite steeply once governments and international agencies gather the political courage to take the measures necessary to constrain global warming emissions.

The workplace

The opposite is true of buildings. Here, the savings to be made are considerable and the payback for energy efficiency measures in particular makes such investment commercially desirable. The design of buildings can also have a significant effect on the efficiency of those working within them. In the UK, the Inland Revenue had to demolish a 19-storey office block in Bootle where half of the 2,000 staff suffered frequently from flu-like symptoms for more than five years due to poor ventilation and a build-up of micro-organisms, usually in heating and ventilating ducts. Some estimates suggest that a third of all office buildings throughout the world suffer from some form of this 'sick building syndrome'.

Research by the UK Building Research Establishment (BRE) has shown that, in general, buildings that are the most energy-efficient are also those that are the most comfortable for the occupants. The combination is not automatic and BRE lists four criteria to be met to achieve the best results:

■ The building must be well-managed, not just in respect of energy but also the entire process of procuring, occupying, operating and maintenance.

■ Conditions must be provided that are within the comfort range of most occupants for most of the time.

■ Facilities must be available to alleviate discomfort quickly when it occurs.

■ Occupants and managers must have ready access to controls for temperature, lighting and ventilation.

Box 9.4 **Halving energy consumption in a building**

The Queen's engineering building at De Montfort University in Leicester – designed by architects Short, Ford with consulting engineers Max Fordham Associates – is one of the largest naturally ventilated buildings in Europe, cutting energy consumption by more than half compared with an equivalent air-conditioned building. It has also been designed and oriented so that, despite its size, natural light penetrates everywhere, reducing the need for artificial light and again cutting energy costs and, therefore, pollution.

This last point is especially important. For example, if occupants have effective control of windows and blinds, then air-conditioning may be unnecessary.

BRE and the PA Consulting Group has published an Environmental Management Toolkit that gives step-by-step guidance on all aspects of the environmental management of buildings, including how to set emission targets and develop and implement remedial action plans. This deals with the environmental impacts of such aspects as the internal environment of a building, the use of resources, energy, transport, noise and neighbourhood issues. The potential advantages for companies and for the environment are considerable. Offices with no previous environmental policy could save up to 20 per cent of their operating costs. The level of greenhouse gas emissions could be reduced dramatically; this would have significant environmental benefits, as the UK's 200,000 offices are responsible for more than 12 per cent of the UK's greenhouse gas emissions.

Key areas in building design

The key areas of concern in building design include high standards of insulation; an efficient heating system; natural ventilation wherever possible; passive temperature control facilities (blinds, heat-reflecting glass and so on); natural lighting wherever possible combined with energy-efficient lighting; and adequate controls both to minimise energy use (lighting that responds to occupancy and switches off when daylight is sufficient) and to provide comfort control for the occupiers. Heat recovery can play a major part in some buildings. For example, supermarkets are now being heated entirely with energy recovered from their food refrigeration systems.

Table 9.1 Energy saving in buildings

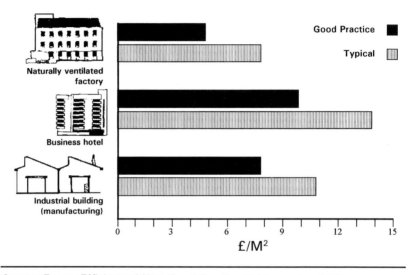

Annual energy consumption in £/M²

Source: Energy Efficiency Office *Good Practice Guide number 136*

The major retail chain Boots has developed a lighting control system for its stores that has cut electricity bills by 65 per cent. Costing £2.5 million to install in 120 stores, the system uses an automatic dimming system and highly efficient light fittings that also give a better quality of light than those they replace. The system is expected to save almost a million pounds a year.

New technology is beginning to offer other ways of cutting pollution and energy bills. In a trial in Newcastle-upon-Tyne – not the world's sunniest city – the cladding on the outside of a university office block has been replaced with panels of photovoltaic solar cells. These provide half of the building's electricity needs in summer and a tenth in winter, powering lighting, computers and other office equipment. The system turns around 17 per cent of solar energy into electricity and has a maximum generating potential of 40 kilowatts. The project is hopelessly uneconomic: the electricity generated over the 30-year life of the panels will cost 45p a unit. However, costs of photovoltaic cells are expected to fall dramatically, while fossil-fuel generated electricity will increase in price, so the Newcastle trial should produce useful practical experience about reliability and maintenance costs that will benefit future users of such systems.

Health

Of course, ensuring the health of occupants is as important as saving energy. Adequate ventilation is essential, as is the avoidance of pollutants that can range from the solvents given off by paints and cleaning fluids to ozone from office copiers and laser printers. Other aspects requiring attention include consideration of the facilities for collecting and sorting waste for recycling; measures to ensure the efficient use of water; and the way in which waste water is treated on site. Landscaping and noise alleviation may also be issues locally.

There is sometimes a risk that well-meaning but heavy-handed bureaucracy may impose rules in the interests of minimising environmental impacts that so constrain designers that the end result may be less than effective. For example, the enhanced Building Regulations introduced in the UK in 1995 and largely aimed at tightening controls on energy consumption include specific rules about the kind of lighting that can be used in commercial buildings. Some interior designers believe that these rules, if imposed without an understanding of the need for special lighting in, for example, an intimate restaurant, will greatly diminish their ability to design effective environments. As a result of representations by the Chartered Institution of Building Services Engineers, the Department of the Environment has issued guidelines on interpreting the regulations aimed at encouraging their sensitive application.

Companies can sometimes fall into the same trap, writing specifications that so inhibit designers and architects that overall effectiveness is constrained. As a general rule, it is better to set specific targets for energy consumption and other environmental indicators than prescribe how the designers should fulfil specific functions.

0 The Green future

■ Introduction ■ Do we really need it? ■ More from less ■ Reducing risk and nuisance ■ Opportunities from technology ■ Concern for nature ■ The transport example ■ A positive future

---

Introduction

Forecasting the future is usually little more than an entertaining diversion, for such forecasts rarely provide any reliable indicator to what happens in practice. So I will resist the temptation to speculate about the kinds of products manufacturers will be making in 50 years time or about the lifestyles that people will adopt in the face of the critical environmental pressures now facing the world.

However, it is possible to discern some of the trends that are likely to be influential in the next ten years. This chapter picks up a few of the developments that are apparent at the time of writing and attempts to draw some conclusions about how these may influence product design as it relates to the environment.

Do we really need it?

'Here we all are struggling to save the world from the Four Horsemen of the Ecological Apocalypse, and it all comes down to defining just what a "green hairspray" might be. Some of us can't help thinking it would be better to do away with hairsprays altogether, green or ungreen. But who are we to precipitate the collapse of western civilisation?' Thus did Jonathan Porritt – one of the UK's leading environmental gurus – sum up what has been called the Deep Green view of consumerism in an article in *Green* magazine in 1993.

So far, this questioning of the need for some of the accepted accoutrements of modern Western culture has been limited to a relatively small sector of the population. This may change. One of the UK's leading commercial environmental consultancies, SustainAbility, certainly thinks so, forecasting that 'In future, promoters of new products will not only need to satisfy the three traditional hurdles of safety, efficiency and quality but also to address the issue of social and economic impacts (the fourth hurdle). The fifth hurdle, we suggest, should address the even trickier issue of need.'

There are indications that some of the world's most important markets may not altogether share the acquisitive aspirations of most Americans and Europeans. Japan, for example, has traditionally been a very frugal society. During 1994, Dentsu – the largest Japanese advertising agency – published several reports suggesting that Japanese consumers were becoming more concerned with personal growth and quality of life. Dentsu identified as one significant trend a growing interest in returning to traditional Japanese values and relatively frugal lifestyles.

Peter James of the Ashridge Management Research Group argues, therefore, that

> Japan may find it easier than any western country to adapt to
> the frugal, ecology-focused lifestyles which may be necessary if
> sustainable development is to be achieved ... There could be
> the creation of a new 'sustainable design' paradigm in which

an explicit environmental component is grafted into the existing national attributes of efficiency, miniaturisation, socialised consumption and technological innovation.[1]

Some major Japanese companies are already changing their view of what their corporate objectives should be in the future. For instance, Ryuzaburo Kaku, Chairman of Canon, believes that the next stage of corporate evolution will be for successful companies to see the entire planet as a stakeholder and seek mutual co-existence with others in order to further sustainable development.

'Temporary pleasure, permanent frustration'

Victor Papanek, the designer whose book *Design for the Real World* inspired the environmental design movement from the moment it was published in the early 1970s, has an interesting view of consumerism. 'People who get no satisfaction out of life (especially from their work) tend to buy things they don't really need in order to get temporary pleasure and permanent frustration – needing ever-more money to insure, repair, replace. If people enjoy life, they need less money', he says.

A reduction in individual purchasing power could also result from more mainstream Green pressures. For example, a study commissioned by the Dutch government has suggested that environmental pressures to improve energy efficiency may result in some activities currently carried out at home being transferred to a large central facility offering economies of scale The study suggests, for instance, that families may choose to eat out at a restaurant to save on the energy needed for cooking and dishwashing or that clothes washing could be transferred to a collect-and-deliver service that would utilise the most energy- and water-efficient appliances to minimise its costs.[2] Technological innovation may itself displace products. This is especially likely to be true with information technology: for example, individual answerphones are already being replaced by a service provided by the phone provider, while the hire of individual films on video is being replaced by films available on demand 'down the line'.

Any sudden or dramatic change to a 'do I really need this product?' attitude is highly unlikely. But there is a deep-seated admiration for thrift in most people (which partly explains the almost universal popularity of recycling) and manufacturers should be aware that a subtle change in people's attitudes to consuming products towards a more economical approach is likely in the future. This may drive a move towards companies being less oriented towards manufacturing and selling products and switching instead to selling an equivalent service. Thus a company may stop selling fridges and freezers and instead provide a food-preservation service that makes profits not from the outright sale of appliances but from a regular service fee charged for providing all of the facilities needed to store food, with long-life appliances being upgraded or repaired as necessary as part of that service.

More from less

The economical approach to consuming is already apparent in areas where resource use has a direct and obvious link to environmental damage. This is especially true of energy but applies to water and other resources too.

This trend towards the ever more efficient use of resources will be intensified for consumer products by the knock-on effect of action elsewhere in the economy. For many products, the housing market is of key importance. So the introduction in 1995 by the Building Research Establishment of an Environmental Standard for housing that sets targets well in excess of even the latest government building regulations and that takes into account the environmental impacts of some of the consumer products installed in a house is significant for some manufacturers. Among the criteria that can help builders achieve the standard are:

- The specification of low-energy lighting in the kitchen, hall, landing, bathrooms and living rooms.
- Provision for a gas cooker (as being more environmentally-friendly than an electric one).
- Provision of a set of four containers for household waste to assist recycling.
- Specifying toilets with a flushing capacity of 6 litres or less.
- Specifying a rain-water collection butt.

The Standard provides a more general impetus towards energy saving products too. One of the mandatory criteria that a house has to meet is a maximum annual carbon dioxide emission level for a given floor area, with an incentive provided to meet an even lower level. This puts a premium not only on designing the house to high insulation standards but encourages the use of, for example, ventilation units that incorporate heat recovery. There is a suggestion that, when the standard is reviewed, one of the additional requirements will be that the light fittings are designed so that only low-energy bulbs can be used. The Building Research Establishment has produced similar environmental standards for offices, supermarkets and other commercial and industrial buildings.

This is just one example of the opportunities for manufacturers who develop products that achieve the efficiency ideal of delivering more from less.

Reducing risk and nuisance

Another area where it is possible to predict with some certainty opportunities for product innovation is that of safety and nuisance. This is partly due to the growing awareness of governments and the public of the damage being caused to health by some of the environmental impacts of modern life and partly to changes in society creating new problems. Occasionally, new problems are created by actions driven by environmental considerations: worries about radon in homes where the geological conditions emit the gas have led to government action mainly because higher standards of home insulation reduce ventilation and thus allow concentrations to build up to potentially damaging levels.

Noise

One environmental nuisance that is moving rapidly up the agenda for action is noise. More than half the homes in England and Wales are exposed to daytime noise that exceeds the World Health Organisation's recommendations; at night, this percentage rises to 63 per cent. The main source of the nuisance is road traffic, but noise from neighbours, from lawnmowers and other powered garden equipment, and from televisions, radios and hi-fis all feature as causes of complaint. While the obvious antidote of improved noise insulation for homes will come, action to reduce noise at source is likely too.

Traffic noise is likely to be tackled in two stages. Road surface materials that halve tyre noise are already available and are likely to be introduced in sensitive areas – for example, where a bypass is sited close to homes and the tyre noise from high-speed traffic is the main source of the nuisance. Of course, the reduction of tyre noise will have the effect of highlighting the noise from vehicle engines, so attention will then move to quietening these too. Noise cancelling techniques – where the noise is analysed and a frequency generated to cancel the effect – are already being used in some vehicles and the technology may be developed for dealing with other noise sources too. The need to quieten vehicles, especially in towns, may give an added impetus to the introduction of electric vehicles, although the prime motivation is the need to reduce local pollution from the exhausts of conventionally-powered vehicles. An experiment by the police using electric cars to reduce pollution has already shown the noise benefit: criminals did not hear the police coming.

The emphasis on noise reduction is likely to affect manufacturers of all kinds of products used outdoors, with higher standards being imposed on everything from garden machinery to equipment used on building sites. Significantly, noise levels are already indicated on the new European Union energy label for domestic appliances.

New pollution worries

While noise has already been targeted for government action, persistent worries about damage to health caused by electro-magnetic radiation from electricity cables have been dismissed by the UK government. However, research is continuing and fears remain, so it is possible that manufacturers of at least some kinds of electrical equipment may in the future be faced with new regulations on the lines of those imposed to restrict radiation from computer monitors.

Alternatives to devices that have the potential to damage health are, of course, always in demand. One example followed the highly successful introduction of *My Lil' Lights* trainers in the

United States. The shoes were the delight of young people, as they lit up every time the heels hit the ground. Then they ran into trouble with environmental protesters when it was discovered that the trainers used mercury – which is toxic and persists in the environment – to complete the electrical circuit that switches on the light. After two states had banned the shoes – despite a recycling programme set up by the manufacturers to recover the mercury – an alternative switch using ball bearings was developed.

Increasing concerns about pollution have created huge markets for monitoring equipment to check everything from pollution in rivers to air quality. It seems likely that technological advances and the growing concern among some of the public about pollution will lead to a demand for monitoring equipment cheap and simple enough to be used domestically, probably primarily for checking air quality.

There is little doubt that the growing awareness of the links between environmental pollution and human health will change perceptions of some products and drive innovation in the future.

Opportunities from technology

With enormous resources being devoted in laboratories around the world to seeking ways of minimising environmental damage, it is hardly surprising that a wide range of new technologies are being generated that seem likely to feed design development in the near future. It is, of course, impossible to describe even a fraction of such developments here. So I will select a few to illustrate some of the ways that environmentally-driven technological development is likely to influence product design (see Box 10.1).

Box 10.1 The UK Technology Foresight programme

The UK Office of Science and Technology (part of the Cabinet Office) has organised a programme aimed at identifying opportunities in marketing and technologies that are likely to emerge in the next 10–20 years. The Technology Foresight Programme is based on research by panels working in 15 sectors ranging from agriculture and chemicals to retail distribution and transport. Altogether, more than 10,000 people have been involved in the programme, whose first results were published in 1995.

Almost all of the sector panels gave priority to some aspect of the environment. Examples include:

IT and electronics panel
■ Encourage the development of new multidiscipline, content-based electronic businesses including tele-medicine, tele-healthcare, remote learning, environmental monitoring and control etc.

Materials panel
■ Processing technologies which improve the environment.
■ Weight-saving technologies for specific applications.

Manufacturing, production and business processes panel
■ Develop process, plant and equipment which meet future environmental needs.

Transport panel
All three key recommendations of this panel were related to environmental issues: using information technology to provide integrated real-time information; developing vehicles which satisfy stringent environmental requirements; and creating more livable urban centres. Specific technologies highlighted were:
■ High strength, lightweight materials.
■ Safety critical systems.
■ Fuel efficient, low emission power plants and energy recovery systems.
■ Quieter vehicles.
■ Accurate location systems.
■ Pattern processing and recognition technologies.

I will begin by looking at two product areas – domestic appliances and lighting – to show the breadth of innovation in key energy-consuming fields. The following are just three examples of innovations that may feed through into domestic appliances soon:

- The American Los Alamos Laboratory has developed a refrigerator that uses sound to compress the refrigerant in place of the conventional piston pump. The invention has a double environmental advantage: the lack of a piston means that the lubricating quality of CFCs is not needed and a non-ozone-depleting gas can be used instead; and the system cuts energy consumption by as much as 40 per cent.

- The French company Welcom International has experimented with specially designed balls for use in a washing machine to simulate a scrubbing action. This enables clothes to be cleaned using half the usual detergent; however, the system damages woollen clothes.

- A clothes dryer that uses microwaves has been tested in the United States. It uses at least 25 per cent less energy than a conventional electric dryer, a reduction with significant environmental benefits as more than 3 million electric dryers are sold in the USA every year.

The rate of innovation in lighting is impressive too:

- Scientists at Queensland University of Technology in Australia have designed light guides that can pipe daylight to provide normal lighting up to 15 metres in from a window, reducing the need for artificial lighting.

- An American company, Fusion Lighting, has developed a revolutionary light source no larger than a golf ball that could massively reduce the energy needed to light large spaces. The light bulbs are filled with a mixture of sulphur and argon which, when bombarded with microwaves, emit a bright light similar in quality to sunlight. In a trial at the headquarters of the American Department of Energy in Washington, two of the new sulphur bulbs were used to replace two hundred and forty 175-watt mercury lamps. Light from the high-intensity bulbs is guided in a light pipe to spread the illumination. Energy savings of around 60 per cent can be achieved by the system.

■ GE Lighting in the United States has used compact fluorescent technology to produce a low energy, long-life bulb shaped like a conventional tungsten bulb, making it easier for people to use compact fluorescents in existing fittings.

Considerable research is also being devoted to improving solar cells, extending their potential well beyond the uses to which they are already being put (mainly where comparatively little power is needed at a site remote from a mains supply, such as garden lights and navigation buoys). Sunlight provides, at its maximum, some 200 watts of energy per square metre but solar cells are never likely to capture anything approaching that level, current cells delivering around 15 per cent of that potential. But efficiencies are improving: Imperial College researchers in London, for example, have developed a 'quantum cell' technique for enhancing the efficiency of solar cells. The device uses an ultra-thin layer of one semi-conductor sandwiched between two layers of another, with the choice of materials and 'band gap' being critical to efficiency. In laboratory trials, the researchers have achieved an efficiency of 25 per cent.

A different approach has been taken by the Swiss Federal Institute of Technology, which has developed transparent solar

---

Box 10.2 **Photovoltaics power an English home**

Half of the roof of a house built in the mid-1990s by a lecturer in architecture in Oxfordshire are covered by photovoltaic cells, producing a maximum of 3 kilowatts, enough to power all the home's electrical equipment, recharge an electric car and still leave some to spare to sell to the national grid. In winter, the cells are augmented from the grid. The designer expects net annual electricity bills of just £10.

cells that can convert 10 per cent of solar energy into electricity. These have the advantage that they could be used on windows without cutting out light. They are already being used to power watches and are cheap to manufacture. In Germany, solar power is being used as a matter of course in all kinds of street furniture, from the lighting of bus shelters and traffic warning signs to powering parking ticket machines. In the United States, the National Institute of Standards and Technology has patented a solar-powered water heater using photovoltaic technology that could halve the cost of domestic installations and provide almost two-thirds of all the domestic hot water needs of homes in the USA.

There are numerous other developments taking place aimed at minimising the use of non-renewable energy and, therefore, pollution. Taxan, for instance, has developed a high quality liquid crystal display colour monitor using thin film transistor active matrix technology that can reproduce 4,090 colours to VGA standard and that consumes just 15 watts of power. The German

---

Box 10.3 Not all high-tech

The EcoLogic Active Insulation Panel demonstrates how a low-tech, simple design approach can achieve substantial environmental and economic gains. Made by Logic Engineering and Manufacturing Ltd, the panel is used behind radiators to achieve a heating efficiency gain of between 15 and 20 per cent, providing a payback period to the user of less than a year. The panel works in three ways. A reflective finish returns radiant heat to the radiator; deep horizontal profiles trap still air to provide an excellent thermal barrier that – with the reflector – drastically reduces heat loss to the wall; and the profiles are designed to create turbulence in the rising hot air behind the radiator, thus accelerating the convective flow and creating a more even distribution of heat in the room. The panel has been designed for easy fitting without removing the radiator using double-sided adhesive tape; the panels are made from metallised PVC and can easily be cut to size.

company Ficht has succeeded in developing the first practical fuel injection system for two-stroke petrol engines. This brings substantial environmental advantages, cutting hydrocarbon emissions by up to 90 per cent, reducing carbon monoxide emissions by 75 per cent, and improving fuel efficiency by a third. Two-stroke piston engines work twice as fast as four-stroke engines, so the injection system has to inject fuel at a higher pressure and more quickly. The Ficht system uses a small piston driven by an electromagnet to squirt the fuel through the injection nozzle at high speed, the magnet being controlled by a microprocessor. Soon after its launch in 1994, Ficht won a contract to equip all the outboard motors used by the Outboard Marine Corporation of Illinois, which makes more than half of the outboard motors sold in the USA.

Rechargeable battery technology is improving rapidly, driven by the demands of the motor industry confronted with the need to develop electric vehicles to meet increasingly harsh emissions standards and by the requirements of mobile phone and computer users. An American company, Ultralife Batteries, has developed the world's first rechargeable battery made entirely from lightweight solid materials. The battery, which uses lithium-based electrodes and a solid polymer-electrolyte whose composition is secret, stores three times as much power weight-for-weight than a conventional nickel-cadmium battery and, because it is solid, is extremely safe. What is more, it can be made in any shape and will sell for the same price as a nickel-cadmium battery and less than conventional lithium batteries.

Another innovation that will help users of battery-powered equipment is a system for accurately warning when a battery is running out of power. A standard for smart battery technology has been agreed by Duracell and Intel which enables battery performance and history to be computed so that battery condition can be checked to an accuracy of 1 per cent. The system helps the battery give up to 20 per cent more working charge, as well as stopping sudden and embarrassing failures.

Smart technology

So-called smart technology seems likely to be a major future influence. It is already appearing in some unlikely products. For example, the Californian company Reliant Technologies has developed smart sunglasses that warn users when they have been exposed to the maximum recommended ultraviolet radiation from sunlight. Photosensors in the frame monitor exposure and a microprocessor calculates the levels received, generating a signal when the maximum is reached that either changes the colour of the spectacles or makes the glasses flicker between dark and clear to warn the wearer.

Smart materials – materials that change their behaviour in response to given criteria – are developing fast and open up all kinds of possibilities. Suggestions range from building materials that 'breathe' fresh air into a home or office when they detect increasing levels of air pollution to clothes that change colour depending on the temperature or wallpaper that can change the décor to suit the occupants' mood.

Miniaturisation

Miniaturisation is a trend that has already had a huge impact on product design and that seems likely to continue to open up possibilities for new products. One development currently being examined is the possibility of heat pumps that are so thin that they could be papered to the wall, providing extremely efficient heating and cooling.

Opportunities range from genetic engineering to biodegradability

I will give just three further examples to illustrate the breadth of technological development that is taking place in response to environmental concerns:

■ Re-using photocopied paper without going through the recycling process may seem unlikely, yet the Japanese manufacturer Ricoh has developed a prototype reverse photocopier that removes the image from photocopies and allows paper to be re-used up to ten times. The paper is sprayed with a 'peel-off' solution and is heated to loosen the toner, which is then lifted off the paper. This is likely to be especially useful for confidential documents, where the only alternative is shredding – a process that makes the paper unsuitable for recycling as the fibres are cut too short. Ricoh has ten patents on the technology.

■ Dyes are often hazardous and the process polluting. Alternatives are now being developed in the form of cotton bred to produce bolls to specific colours. Machine-spinnable browns and greens are already being grown and plants bred to produce a range of other colours are being developed. But blue has proved unachievable through normal plant-breeding techniques, so an American genetic company, Agracetus, is using genetic engineering techniques to insert into cotton plants the genes that produce the blue colour in the indigo plant. Advances in genetic engineering are likely to provide product designers with solutions to many more environmental problems in the future.

■ The UK Patent Office is just one of many institutions that recognise the need for designers to take more account of environmental factors that are playing their part in enabling progress. For example, the Patent Office has published a monograph on *Environmentally Degradable Polymers* giving details of a wide range of patents for throw-away degradable products. Ideas range from packaging and toothbrushes to razor blades and coffins.

Concern for nature

Animal welfare is high on the agenda of some environmentalists and this, again, is already providing a stimulus for product development. One example is some work carried out at the Royal College of Art in London that resulted in the marketing of two products aimed at improving the welfare of pigs. The first was a new design of pig feeder that prevents pigs from seeing each other while eating, so discouraging aggression; the second was an alternative to the traditional farrowing crate for sows which allows the sow to behave naturally while protecting the piglets from accidental damage.

Innovative design has also been used to reduce the quantity of pesticides used on farms. One example is the Bug-Vac, a device developed in California that works like a vacuum cleaner, sucking pests off crops such as strawberries and thus avoiding the need for pesticides. It is being sold in Europe as well as the United States.

Concern for wild animals has also encouraged product development. Worries about the number of deer and other animals killed on roads – and about the damage that collisions with deer and other larger animals can cause to cars and their occupants – has led to the development of 'wolves eyes' that use the principle of the cat's eye to reflect car headlights sideways into the adjacent countryside. An experiment in Cannock Chase in the UK has shown the system to be effective in stopping deer from crossing the road, although there has been a consequential rise in collisions in the period immediately after dawn.

Even dolphins have inspired product development. When the world maritime regulations were amended in 1989 to ban the dumping of all plastics refuse at sea after dolphins and other large animals had been killed by eating such rubbish, golf on board cruise ships was one of the first casualties. But a San Diego inventor solved the problem by designing a water-soluble golf ball. The ball – which behaves in the same way as an ordinary golf ball – uses paper pulp bound together with gelatin for the outer skin in place of plastic and a mixture of sodium bicarbonate and sodium citrate in place of the usual liquid rubber core.

The transport example

I will end by looking at some of the trends in transport, the industry that heads the list of those challenged to change by environmental issues. For the problems and opportunities for change within transport encapsulate those that are likely to affect every business in the move towards a sustainable economic and environmental system.

As I have explained before, lateral solutions to environmental problems are sometimes the best. One of the lateral solutions to transport pollution and congestion is to avoid transport altogether. One way of achieving this is, of course, by utilising information technologies as envisaged by the UK Technology Foresight Programme. This is already beginning to make a significant impact, both in encouraging more people to work at least partly from home or from local telecottages and by reducing the need to travel to meetings. The scope for travel reduction is large: a report by US Federal Aviation Administration and the

Massachusetts Port Authority predicted that between 13 and 23 per cent of business travel from Boston's Logan airport may be replaced by videoconferencing by 2010. Many of the initial fears about teleworking have proved unfounded – for instance, there were concerns that people working from home, especially in rural areas, would suffer isolation from a lack of social contact. But a study by David Osborne, Professor of Psychology at the University of Swansea, has shown this not to be the case.

Information technology

The information technology revolution seems likely to impact on transport in many other ways too, with teleshopping, dial-up films and education programmes, and many other services currently involving travel being available without moving out of the home. Of course, the impact of such developments will merely reduce car use, not eliminate the need for transport, and, therefore, the impact in product design terms may be more on the providers of the information technology services and equipment, including the development of new purpose-designed domestic-styled furniture and accessories.

Information technology is, of course, already having a more direct impact on transport. For instance, route planning by computer is well-established and interactive on-board route guidance systems that include the ability to find ways round traffic hold-ups are becoming available. Such systems are likely to develop fast and include such features as the ability to guide a driver to the nearest empty parking space in a city centre, thus saving much time and fuel. The day when such systems take over the driver's job altogether may only be delayed by public distrust of its safety and by the pleasure that many people get from driving. However, unless the death and injury toll of road accidents caused by driver error plummets – an unlikely scenario – then it may not be too far into the twenty-first century before automated driving becomes the norm.

In the meantime, safety considerations are already inspiring a use for new technology. Daimler-Benz, for instance, filed a patent early in 1995 for a car that detects whether there is a safe gap for overtaking. The vehicle uses radar to monitor the space behind, beside and in front of the car, the information being compared with the driver's reaction time and the car's performance to indicate to the driver whether the overtaking manoeuvre is safe or not.

Noise reduction

New technology to reduce the noise inside a car has already been introduced. In 1992, Nissan became the first manufacturer to use noise cancelling technology. The system, introduced in Nissan's Bluebird model, analyses the sound waves from the engine and generates a mirror image of these waves, thus cancelling out the noise. The system cuts noise by around ten decibels, enabling a reduction in soundproofing materials (which account for around 30 kg in an average car) and thus helping to improve fuel efficiency too.

Reducing pollution and increasing fuel efficiency

Of course, the most attention is being paid to reducing pollution and improving fuel efficiency. This has led to research programmes across the spectrum of vehicle design, from new materials aimed at reducing the weight of cars or improve engine performance to new energy sources and regenerative braking systems.

The scale and variety of investigation is illustrated by the following small selection of examples and by the motorcycle design shown in Figure 10.1:

■ Amory Lovins, Director of the respected Rocky Mountain Institute in Colorado, has suggested that a hybrid fuel electric car with a lightweight body made from carbon fibre could achieve a performance of at least 150 miles per gallon of fuel.

■ Chrysler has designed a racing car that combines a gas turbine engine driving the wheels through electric motors; the gas turbine runs at a steady speed and when generating surplus power this is fed into a high-speed flywheel to store the energy for use when required. The car, which was entered for the 1995 Le Mans 24-hour race, is intended to demonstrate that a comparatively clean and efficient vehicle need not be boring.

■ The winner of the 1993 3,000 km Darwin to Adelaide race for solar-powered cars was won at an average speed of 85 kph and a top speed of 125 kph.

■ An American company, Pneumacom, has built a zero-emission prototype car powered by compressed air. It has a top speed of around 60 kph and one charge lasts around two hours.

Figure 10.1 Advanced motorcycle cuts pollution

The design consultancy Seymour Powell has developed this 'Nexus' motorcycle concept to take advantage of advanced bicycle technology and state-of-the-art motorcycle engine technology to produce a fast and very efficient lightweight motorcycle for urban use. The chassis is a carbon-fibre reinforced monocoque that provides great strength and lightness while providing cavities for fuel and the ignition electronics. The advanced three horsepower ceramic two-stroke engine burns petrol at a very high temperature to minimise polluting emissions. Fuel consumption in the region of 150 miles per gallon is expected, with a top speed of around 40 mph. (Seymour Powell.)

■ Researchers at the University of Newcastle-upon-Tyne have developed fuel cells that run on methanol. The ultra-efficient cells generate electricity through a chemical reaction and may be especially suitable for powering cars of the future, as methanol is easier and safer to use than the usual alternative, hydrogen.

■ Japanese engineers have designed an engine that burns methanol directly, giving pollution advantages over petrol engines. Methanol has not been used commercially before because it is toxic and corrodes metal engines. The Japanese team – backed by Isuzu, a major bus and lorry manufacturer – has overcome the problems by designing an engine made from ceramics that, partly because of the heat-retention properties of the material, operates at 38 per cent efficiency compared with the 30 per cent usually achieved by petrol engines.

These developments are seen as essential for the future of the car manufacturing industry in order to avoid the heavy hand of the environmentalists and the legislators. It is not only technological developments that will lead to new design opportunities. The UK Society of Motor Manufacturers and Traders (SMMT) has forecast that environmental factors will force many users to buy different cars for different purposes: 'In the next century we will see more families with perhaps three cars for different reasons – an electric vehicle for city use, an inter-city car and a weekend leisure vehicle', said the SMMT in 1994. That view horrifies deep Green eco-enthusiasts. But the view that environmental solutions are likely to come from new product development and design improvement is, in the short term at least, more practicable and more achievable than the fundamental change in lifestyle desired by the deep Greens.

Lessons for all product developers

What is happening in the transport industry highlights the main issues that can face manufacturers and their product development teams in any industry:

■ Tightening environmental regulations are forcing the development of cleaner and more efficient engines, as well as driving the development of such add-on devices as catalytic converters and exhaust filters. This is being paralleled in other sectors with the development of products that are more efficient and with add-on clean-up equipment.

■ Environmental forces are driving the development of novel solutions. In the case of the motor industry, this is initially mainly in the form of electric vehicles but includes research into other types of fuel. In turn, these developments offer opportunities for product innovation in the related support services (see Figure 10.2).

■ Although technological developments are often necessary in achieving environmental advantage, the design of the interfaces with the user of the product are critical in realising the full benefits.

■ The environmental problems of one industry can open up substantial opportunities for new products and services provided by entirely different technologies or industries.

■ Successful design for the environment requires both attention to detail – lightweighting, ensuring ease of maintenance and disassembly and so on – and an awareness of potential lateral solutions.

A positive future

Some companies and managers see environmental pressures as

An example of how environmental pressures are creating a demand for new kinds of product is the way that concern about urban pollution is forcing car manufacturers to develop electric vehicles. This, in turn, is creating a need for entirely new products, such as this electric vehicle charging station designed in the United States by IDEO and Ciro Design for General Motors and Hughes Electronics. The scheme won a 1995 *Business Week*/Industrial Designers Society of America Gold Award. (IDEO.)

Figure 10.2 **Electric vehicle charging station**

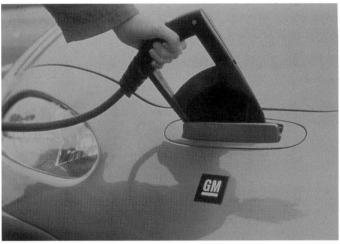

negative – adding cost, presenting problems, generating difficult-to-manage situations and best evaded. I hope that this book has demonstrated that such an approach is both unwarranted and commercially unsustainable. For most manufacturing companies, environmental issues are now unavoidable and are a necessary part of a design team's brief.

But design for the environment is far more positive than that. It is implicitly linked to gaining the maximum efficiency in the use of resources both in manufacturing and use, thus offering advantages to the producer and the customer. It is entirely compatible with Total Quality Management. It can improve performance in existing markets and open up entirely new markets. Above all, design for the environment is a tool that, properly managed, can improve profitability and competitiveness.

References

Chapter 1

1. Manus van Brakel (1992), 'Overview of Sustainable Consumption and Environmental Space' in *Consumers and the Environment*, Penang: International Organisation of Consumers Union.
2. World Commission on Environment and Development (1987), *Our Common Future*, Oxford: Oxford University Press.
3. Mintel (1994), *The Green Consumer*, London: Mintel.
4. Central Statistical Office (1994), *Social Focus on Children*, London: Central Statistical Office.

Chapter 2

1. Australian Manufacturing Council (1993), *The Environmental Challenge: Best Practice Environmental Regulation*, Melbourne: Australian Manufacturing Council.
2. *Environmental Business Magazine*, April 1995.
3. Paper by David Cope, Peter James, Emiko Kusakabe and Jonathan Selwyn, Centre for Environment and Economic Development, Ashridge Management Research College, to the *From Greening to Sustaining* conference organised by the Greening of Industry Network in Denmark, November 1994.
4. Association of British Chambers of Commerce (1994), *Small Firms Survey: Environment*, London: Association of British Chambers of Commerce.
5. ACBE (1994), *Fourth Progress Report*, London: Department of

Trade and Industry.

6. *Independent,* 29 September 1992.

7. *Public Treasurer,* January 1995.

Chapter 3

1. *Products and the Environment* (1994), The Hague: Ministry of Housing.

2. US Congress, Office of Technology Assessment (1992), *Green Products by Design,* Washington DC: US Government Printing Office.

3. Jonathan Williams (1994), Briefing for RSA workshop on *Environmental Design in the Telecommunications Industry,* March 1994.

4. Stephen Potter and Robin Roy (1994), *Ecodesign Management: A Comparative Study,* Milton Keynes: Open University Design Innovation Group.

5. S.A. Bush (1993), *Designing for Whole Life Cost,* Coventry University Centre for Integrated Design.

6. Ibid.

7. *Products and the Environment* (1994), The Hague: Ministry of Housing.

Chapter 5

1. Dorothy Mackenzie (1991), *Green Design – Design for the Environment,* London: Laurence King.

2. New Economics Foundation (1994), *Beyond Recycling,* London: New Economics Foundation.

3. Leonard Oberascher, Oko-Psy, Austria, speaking at the Nunspeet *Design for the Environment* conference in the Netherlands in 1992.

Chapter 7

1. Peter James and Martin Bennett (1994), *Environment-related Performance Measurement in Business*, Berkhamsted: Ashridge Management Research Group.

Chapter 8

1. National Consumer Council (1989), *The Consumer Guarantee*, London: National Consumer Council.

Chapter 10

1. Peter James (1994), *Environment by Accident, Sustainability by Design?*, paper presented to the *Greening of Industry* conference, Copenhagen (based on research by the Ashridge Management Research Group).
2. Environmental Resources Management (1993), *The Best of Both Worlds: Sustainability and Quality Lifestyles in the 21st Century*, The Hague: Directorate-General for the Environment.

Appendix: sources of further information

Listed here are some of the sources of information that may be especially useful to manufacturers and product developers wishing to incorporate environmental factors into their activities. This information was correct in July 1995, as far as it was possible to check. It is not intended to be comprehensive and may be of most use treated simply as a starting point.

Information is given under the following headings:

- Buildings
- Design
- Energy
- Environmental performance measures
- Environmental pressure groups
- Environmental regulations
- Environmental technology
- General
- Financial assistance
- Lifecycle analysis
- Products
- Recycling

At the end, a list is included of some books and magazines that may be helpful.

Buildings

The *Building Research Establishment* provides a whole range of publications, software programs and other helpful material related to buildings, covering design, construction and use. Building Research Establishment, Garston, Watford WD2 7JR (phone: +44 1923 894040; fax: +44 1923 664099).

The Office Toolkit referred to on page 171 is available from CRC Ltd, 33–39 Bowling Green Lane, London EC1R 0DA (phone: +44 1923 64444).

Design

The *UK Design Council* has a national strategic role as a design authority informing and complementing the work of local providers of services such as the Business Links network and educational institutions. It publishes the quarterly magazine *DESIGN* and undertakes research projects, including some relating to design and the environment. Design Council, Haymarket House, 1 Oxendon Street, London SW1Y 4EE (phone +44 171 208 2121; fax +44 171 839 6036).

The *UK Ecological Design Association* aims to link designers globally to provide information, education and the exchange of ideas. It publishes a quarterly journal *EcoDesign* and holds regular meetings and an annual weekend seminar. Ecological Design Association, The British School, Slad Road, Stroud, Gloucestershire GL5 1QW (phone +44 1453 765575; fax +44 1453 759211).

The *Centre for Sustainable Design* has been set up within the Faculty of Design at the Surrey Institute of Art and Design. It aims to facilitate discussion and research, with activities ranging from training, seminars, publications and information services. The Centre can be contacted at The Surrey Institute of Art & Design, Falkner Road, Farnham, Surrey GU9 7DS (phone: +44 1252 73229; fax: +44 1252 732274; email: csfd@surrart.ac.uk).

Energy

The *Sesame Database* contains technical and administrative information on energy research and development projects. Run online by the German STN organisation, it is available in CD-ROM format in the UK from Longman (phone: +44 1279 623928).

The government *Energy Efficiency Office* publishes extensive information about best energy efficiency practice in various industries and about technological developments. It runs a free Helpline and provides some financial support for research and development. It also funds a special scheme to assist small businesses participate in the EU Ecomanagement and Audit Scheme. Energy Efficiency Office, Department of the Environment, 2 Marsham Street, London SW1P 3EB (phone: +44 171 276 6200; fax: +44 171 298 3318).

Environmental performance measures

Business in the Environment and KPMG Peat Marwick's National Environment Unit have produced a guidebook – *A Measure of Commitment – Guidelines for Measuring Environmental Performance* – on environmental performance measures illustrated by case studies from 14 companies (see Business in the Environment under 'General' below).

Environmental pressure groups

Friends of the Earth is the leading general environmental pressure group and usually takes a reasoned and fact-based approach to its campaigns. It publishes a range of reports, some of which are relevant to manufacturers. Friends of the Earth, 26–28 Underwood Street, London N1 7JQ (phone: +44 171 490 1555).

Greenpeace concentrates its campaigns on a fairly narrow range of issues, of which its energy campaigning is likely to be of most interest to designers. Greenpeace, Canonbury Villas, London N1 2PN (phone: +44 171 354 5100).

The *Women's Environmental Network* specialises in giving advice about environmental issues and products – sometimes from a highly tendentious viewpoint. Women's Environmental Network, Aberdeen Studios, 22 Highbury Grove, London N5 2EA (phone: +44 171 354 8823).

GreenNet is not strictly a pressure group. But this global computer communications network operates as a chatline for Green enthusiasts and presents an opportunity to establish a range of opinions on current topics. GreenNet, 393–395 City Road, London EC1V 1NE (phone: +44 171 713 1941; fax: +44 171 833 1169; email: support@gn.apc.org).

Environmental regulations

The *Engineering Employers Federation* publishes a Register of Environmental Regulations which outlines the significant environmental legislation and official guidance affecting the manufacturing sector in England and Wales. It is likely to be particularly helpful to SMEs considering participating in environmental management schemes such as BS 7750 or EMAS by helping them draw up an appropriate register for their own businesses. Headings include: air, water, waste and hazardous substances. Engineering Employers Federation, Broadway House, Tothill Street, London SW1H 9NQ (phone: +44 171 222 7777; fax: +44 171 222 2782).

Full information on relevant British Standards, Health and Safety legislation, and official guidance notes is available on a CD-ROM or online from *SilverPlatter Information* under the title 'OSH-UK'; this is published as a joint venture with HMSO. SilverPlatter also publishes 'Toxline', a database that includes information on the interactions between chemical substances and biological systems; environmental pollution; occupational health; waste disposal etc. SilverPlatter Information Ltd, 10 Barley Mow Passage, Chiswick, London W4 4PH (phone: +44 181 995 8242; fax: +44 181 995 5159).

The 'Pharos' software for PCs has been developed by the *National Westminster Bank* to provide information on the European Single Market and environmental legislation and business issues. It is interactive, enabling a company to build up a review of business issues ranging from the Single European Market to environmental legislation. 'Pharos' is available free to NatWest customers. National Westminster Bank, 41 Lothbury, London EC2P 2BP.

Environmental technology

The *Environmental Technology Best Practice Programme* is run jointly in the UK by the Department of Trade and Industry and the Department of the Environment. The prime aims are to promote waste minimisation and cost-effective cleaner technology through technology transfer. Services include environmental performance guides giving bench-marking data for specific industry sectors and technologies; good practice guides; information about new practice; and financial support for the research and development of innovative environmental technologies. Initial access to the Programme is via the UK freephone number 0800 585794.

General

Business in the Environment was set up to help UK companies, particularly small and medium-sized firms, meet environmental challenges. It publishes a variety of useful guides, including a directory of organisations providing advice at a local level. Business in the Environment, 8 Stratton Street, London W1X 5FD (phone: +44 171 629 1600; fax: +44 171 629 1834).

The British Library runs an environmental information service to track down information on environmental subjects, including pollution, clean technologies, and commercial and legal aspects. Environmental Information Service, The British Library, 25 Southampton Buildings, London WC2A 1AW (phone: +44 171 412 7955; fax: +44 171 412 7954).

Cambridge Scientific Abstracts produces CD-ROM environmental management disks providing abstracts across the environmental sciences from some 7,000 sources covering pollution, environmental action, ecosystems analysis, pesticides, radiation, toxic hazards, waste treatment and water treatment. Available from Dialog Information Services, 3460 Hillview Avenue, Palo Alto, California CA 94304-1396, USA (phone: +1 415 858 3785; fax: +1 415 858 6350).

The *Greening of Industry Network* organises conferences, reports and promotes research and information exchange on policies for a sustainable future. Greening of Industry Network, Centre for Studies of Science, Technology and Society, TWr.RC 302, PO Box 217, University of Twente, 7500 A E Enschede, The Netherlands (phone: +31 53 89 3344; fax: +31 53 35 0625; email: schot%fwt%wmw@civp.utwente.nl).

The UK government has set up an organisation to assist the marketing of environmental products and services overseas. Called the *Joint Environmental Markets Unit*, it can be contacted at: Department of Trade and Industry, 1 Victoria St, London SW1H 0ET (phone: +44 171 215 2742).

The *European Information Centre for Environmental Matters*

(NETT) is a non-profit information centre backed by the European Commission. It offers three services in exchange for an annual fee, an on-line database; a personal inquiry service; and an electronic 'meeting' service with other members. NETT, Avenue Louise 207, Box 10, 1050 Bruxelles (phone: +32 2645 0940; fax: +32 2646 4266).

There are more than 200 *European Information Centres* throughout Europe, including 24 in the UK. They provide information for businesses about all relevant aspects of European Union legislation and activities, including instant information about all EU Law. A full list of the centres is available from the European Commission, Rue de la Loi 200, B-1049 Bruxelles (fax: +32 2 296 4271).

Financial assistance

The *European Union* operates a number of schemes to assist the development of environmental innovative products and services, as well as providing information. European Union (London Office), 8 Storey's Gate, London SW1 (phone: +44 171 973 1992).

Assistance may also be available from government sources in the UK. Information can be obtained through the *Environmental Technology Best Practice Programme* (see above Environmental technology section).

Lifecycle analysis

The *SimaPro* software is available from PRé Consultants, Bergstraat 6, 3811 NH Amersfoort, The Netherlands (phone: +31 33 611046; fax: +31 33 652853).

The *LCA Inventory Tool* software is available from Chalmers Industriteknik, Chalmers Teknipark, S-412 88 Goteborg, Sweden (phone: +46 31 772 4237; fax: +46 31 82 74 21).

The *PEMS* and *EcoAssessor* LCA software are available from PIRA International, Randalls Road, Leatherhead, Surrey KT22 7RU (phone: +44 1372 376161; fax: +44 1372 377526).

Products

Conservation Papers Ltd runs an *Environmental Product Information Centre* (EPIC) to provide a telephone service offering free help to businesses seeking environmentally-preferable products. Of most interest to office users, the service utilises a database to identify the products most likely to match the user's needs; information sheets are then sent out by post. Environmental Product Information Centre, 228 London Road, Reading, Berkshire RG6 1AH (phone: +44 1734 665665; fax: +44 1734 351605).

Recycling

Waste Exchange Services Ltd has a database containing details of over 1.5 million tonnes of wastes available to manufacturers, as well as providing general data on recycling routes. Materials on offer range from crushed egg shells and glass nuggets to polythene foam and GRP sheets. Waste Exchange Services Ltd, 70 Brunswick Street, Stockton-on-Tees, Cleveland TS18 1DW (phone +44 1642 606055; fax +44 1642 603726).

HMSO published a *Recycled Paper Register* in 1994 listing all the products on the market and, more importantly, giving a weighted score for each paper taking into account both the percentage content and the source of recycled fibres. HMSO, 49 High Holborn, London WC1 (phone +44 171 873 0011).

Books and magazines

The book *BS7750 Implementing the Environment Management*

Standard and the EC Eco-Management Scheme, by Brian Rothery and published by Gower in 1993, provides a definitive guide to these important management standards.

Still an excellent introduction to the subject – especially for industrial designers – is Dorothy Mackenzie's 1991 book *Green Design – Design for the Environment*, published by Laurence King.

A report prepared in 1993 by designer Simon Berry provides practical guidelines for product designers about waste reduction, primarily by designing for recycling. The report – which includes case studies of two companies – is of most interest for designers of products with a high plastics content. *Completing the Cycle – Product Design for Recycling* is published by Environmental Product Design, 5 Church Croft, Gargrave, Skipton, North Yorkshire BD23 3NZ (phone +44 1756 748065).

Three books published by Stanley Thornes are relevant. *Business Success from Seizing the Environmental Initiative* by Christine Hemming uses the experience of the PA Consulting Group's Golden Leaf Awards to show how environmental and business objectives can be met in practice. *Improving Environmental Performance* – written by Sara Bragg, Philippa Knapp and Ronald McLean – draws on the experience of the authors' work for a major management consultancy to provide practical guidance for developing environmental management systems. Dr Linda Spedding's book, *International Environmental Policy and Management,* provides a general guide but is particularly useful for companies operating in developing markets, as it contains a rare insight into how environmental regulation is developing in countries such as China, India and Malaysia. Stanley Thornes, Ellenborough House, Wellington Street, Cheltenham, Glouces-tershire GL50 1YD (phone: +44 1242 228888; fax: +44 1242 221914).

A useful overview of current environmental issues is provided by the *ENDS Report*, which is published monthly by Environmental Data Services, 40 Bowling Green Lane, London EC1R 0NE (phone +44 0171 278 4745).

The Green Management Letter provides a monthly briefing for managers, including information about what other companies are doing on the environmental front. Information from Euromanagement, PO Box 2192, 5600 CD Eindhoven, The Netherlands (phone: +31 40 433 577; fax: +31 40 460 885).

The Environment in Europe is published five times a year and is available from the Institute for European Environmental Policy, 3 Endsleigh Street, London WC1H 0DD (phone: +44 0171 388 2117).

Green Design is a quarterly newsletter published by the Canadian-based Sustainable Development Association and covering news, case histories and other information. Subscription details are available from: Sustainable Development Association, 4560 Mariette Avenue, Montreal, Canada H4B 2G2 (email: sda@grndsn.login.qc.ca).

The Manual of Environment Policy is a constantly updated loose-leaf manual written by the Director of the London Office of the Institute of European Environmental Policy. Information is available from the Longman Group UK Ltd, Westgate House, Freepost, Harlow Essex CM20 1YQ (phone: +44 1279 442601).

Index